GREENLAND

Baffin Bay

Thule

Alert

raig Harbour

das Harbour

ound

BYLOT I.

Pond
Inlet

River Clyde

Godhavn

Davis Strait

BAFFIN ISLAND

Pangnirtung

Cumberland Sd.

Frobisher Bay

Cape Dorset

Lake
Harbour

I.

TINGHAM I.

RESOLUTION I.

Hudson St.

BUTTON IS.

Wolstenholme

Wakeham Bay

Port Burwell

Cape Smith

AKPATOK I.

Hebron

Povungnituk

Fort Chimo

George
River

NEWFOUNDLAND

ATLANTIC

OCEAN

Hopedale

Makkovik

Cartwright

Goose Bay

BAY

Shefferville

QUEBEC

L. Wonders

mes

Bay

Corner Brook

Gander

St.
John's

70 60 50 40 30 20

80 70 60

60

40

50

50

GEORGIA
An Arctic Diary

GEORGIA
An Arctic Diary

Hurtig Publishers
Edmonton

Hurtig Publishers
10560 105 Street
Edmonton, Alberta

Canadian Cataloguing in Publication Data

Georgia, 1928-
  Georgia

  ISBN 0-88830-225-8

  1. Georgia, 1928-   2. Inuit — Northwest
Territories — Social life and customs.*
I. Title: Georgia: an Arctic diary.
E99.E7G46   970.004'97   C82-091200-X

Printed and bound in Canada
by T.H. Best Printing Co. Ltd.

Though all events described in my journal actually happened, some of the villagers' names have been changed. The main family groups mentioned are those of INAQ, which includes his parents Itu and Ningiu, his wife Alitsiaq, their children Sally, Johnny, and Natar, and his cousin Pita and wife Letia; TOBY, his wife Sila, and their children Levi, Natika, Tutu, Suzie, Ivo, Abraham, Rebecca, Sita, and Larry; UINGA, his wife Jeannie, their two daughters, and his brothers Timuti and Davidee; OQAK, his wife Siuti, sons Nukinaq, Malak, and Tukilaq, Tukilaq's wife Sara, and sons Jamisi and Alita. Oqak's nephew Jamesi and his wife Kati are included in this family group. Two other families are those of SIMAGAK and Dora and their five children; and TUGALA and Anna and their seven children.

Introduction

Missionaries, some of whom have spent more than forty years living the traditional and now the contemporary life with the Inuit, are the first to protest that they do not know the Inuit. The longer you know them, say the missionaries, the less you understand the Inuit and the less willing you are to predict how they will react in specific situations. What I give here is what I have learned, or what I have observed, how I have reacted, and how I feel in certain situations and in regard to certain aspects of Inuit life around me. I don't presume to "tell the truth about the Inuit." My account is subjective, not scholarly. The same facts can be interpreted in many ways. The life I see around me, the events and non-events I live are subject to interpretation just like any other facts. I hereby serve notice that my interpretation of those facts often consciously leans towards the idyllic rather than the pessimistic.

In the Canadian Arctic today it is possible to live much as any Canadian in southern Canada lives. All the consumer goods, foods, and gadgets available in southern Canada are available in the North through cataloue sales, air freight, and a whimsical postal service. Perhaps these amenities are not as easily acquired or available on short notice as in southern Canada, but the days are gone when northern duty was synonymous with hardship duty. For some members of other cultures, northern life was always a preferred alternative lifestyle, as it is today, but the time when a large stock of courage and stamina were prerequisites for arctic living is gone. It has disappeared with the advent of more frequent and dependable air service, a large fleet of annual resupply ships and ice-breakers, and above all, government interest in and assumption of responsibility for the native residents, with the resultant burgeoning presence of non-Inuit.

The Inuit have leaped into the twentieth century, economically, by becoming members of the consumer society and politically, with a new awareness of their uniqueness. They are now trying to protect that treasured heritage from which their uniqueness springs. It is a fascinating time to be in the North, sometimes exhilarating, often heart-breaking, as people consciously and unconsciously work to fashion a new culture. The future Inuit culture will not be a total return to the traditional ways. Only purists would want men to live under the constant shadow of death by starvation or natural accident, braving the harshest climate on the face of the earth with none of the implements and aids developed by other cultures. I have never heard of a single Inuk, no matter how old or "traditionally minded," who wanted to return to the days when Inuit did not have fuel stoves and outboard motors, let alone firearms. Nor will the future Inuit society be a carbon copy of one of the models proffered. My hope and prayer is that the fruit of the barren-lands may be the happy melding of the best elements of the cultures now struggling for supremacy there.

Since 1970 I have lived in the two barren-lands settlements generally reputed to be the most traditional Canadian Inuit villages. Though I have visited other settlements, my views and opinions are naturally conditioned by the two places I have called home. I strongly sense the continued rapid transition in the North. My first two winters north of the tree line, I did not have electricity and refused to annoy myself trying to decipher short-wave radio emissions. The vagaries of local telephones were such that I preferred to walk myself or use cookies to entice some passing child to deliver local messages. The Hudson's Bay Company, Roman Catholic Mission, and Government of the Northwest Territories radios kept us in touch with "the outside," though the weather could always sever those tenuous threads. Long distance radio-telephone, using the government assigned frequency during specified hours, was, in my opinion, worse than nothing, for it whetted my curiosity as to what the other person was saying but did not satisfy that curiosity since it was impossible for me to comprehend. Personal failing, I am quick to add, for others sometimes employed phones and radio to their satisfaction.

The present was launched in 1972 with Anik satellite. I rejoice in some of the changes it has brought and ruefully accept others. My personal reaction was to have a telephone which not only drew my village neighbours as close as the dial, but allows me to talk with friends in the south — a noticeable psychological boon. The Northern Service of the CBC has radio programming in seven languages from four major centres in the Northwest Territories in addition to southern feed and local radio. Through contemporary reporting of current events throughout the world as well as in the Northwest Territories, the Inuit have been even more profoundly exposed to the cultural influences which have been seeping into the North since the time of the early explorers. Television and the game laws vie with each other as the last straw, mustering hitherto silent or soft-spoken pressure to preserve Inuit culture.

Daily life in any northern settlement presents myriad faces of conflict between old and new, young and old, alien and native. I have made no attempt to deal with these intriguing angles of contemporary life, yet they are the substrata from which spring the facts, attitudes, and episodes that I do treat. Who would ignore the ferment in today's northern society would deny the very existence of that society.

I write facts as I feel them. Someone else will see my realities as myths, the truths I treat as falsehoods. Some will agree with me one hundred per cent, others seventy per cent, and others will toss me onto the heap of northern romanticizers. Quyana!

As there are people who take medicine without reading the instructions on the bottle, there are people who read books without reading their introductions. Let the introduction reader not be disconcerted to find the echo of these sentiments, cautions, and prescriptions reiterated in the pages that follow.

March

21 March

The phone rang.

"Can you see Larry?" I looked out my window, across the snow beyond the two parallel mounds between which the road passes, and scanned the white expanse to Toby's house fifty yards away.

"No," I answered.

"He's coming to visit." Sila chose simple words and spoke slowly so that I might understand her Inuktitut. "This is the first time he has asked to go visiting by himself." Her words came quicker, tinged with excitement. "Can you see him yet?"

"Yes," I answered as a tiny head appeared above the piled up snow on the far side of the road. Because I couldn't find the words I needed, I merely said "Goodbye," hung up, pulled on my parka, and ran out to pick up the two-year-old, not yet big enough to scale the snow-plough's debris. When I put him down on the far side of the street, Larry waddled deliberately towards my house. He had finished a cup of hot chocolate before his mother came to join him.

When I had arrived at Igloolik, Mark Evaluardjuk had asked me to cook at his Tojormivik Hotel — the Transient Centre — and through his good auspices I had been assigned Northern Low Rental House #14. During the renovations necessary to make the "biscuit box" habitable, I had gotten to know Inaq and Pita of the Housing Association work crew, and Toby, chairman of the Board of Directors and father of the little boy, Larry. Since Toby's house was on my way to almost everywhere — the Transient Centre, Hudson's Bay and Co-op stores, post office, churches — I often popped in to visit. As I gradually got to know the family, I felt more and more at home with them.

Toby was forty-one and Sila thirty-eight when I first knew them. Their oldest son, twenty-one-year-old Levi, was working at the Armed Forces Base at Alert. Quiet nineteen-year-old Natika provided much of the meat and fish for the family, also bringing in seal skins and fox furs for his mother to process. His hunting partner was another nineteen-year-old, Tommy. Tutu, the oldest girl, then seventeen, told me in excellent English that all the Igloolik girls wanted Tommy for a boyfriend when he arrived from Arctic Bay. "But," she declared with a proud smile, "I got him!" Suzie, fifteen, intelligent and innovative like her sister, also spoke excellent, though embarassingly profane, English. Next were two boys; heavy-set thirteen-year-old Ivo and slight eleven-year-old Abraham, a budding hunter. Rebecca was nine and Sita five. Larry and I had been recent additions to Toby's family, for they had adopted me as Inuit have taken white men under their wing ever since the first explorers "discovered" the original arctic residents.

Sila and I drank tea and watched the ball game on the ice until about 8:30, when Larry became fretful and they left. In the dusk I counted about thirty players out there, with children on bikes roaming around and through the game, and the motor toboggans of seal hunters, pulling qamutiks, coming and going between the village and the floe edge. Bicycle licenses are the vogue this spring, as are plastic sleds, several of which lay near the beach, abandoned by young ball players.

I could see Itu busy beside his house with his son Inaq and cousin Pita who had reconditioned my house. Itu finished a hunting skiff yesterday and today the two younger men are helping him build a qamutik. Ever since I have lived here, Itu has been the master craftsman, providing harpoon heads, as£unaaq, and other tools to those who ask. I watched fascinated as he worked all last summer fashioning motor fittings, steering cables, and other mysterious parts to refurbish one of the whale boats that had been lying on the beach for years. A respected leader in his camp before the Inuit moved into the settlement, Itu retains that respect in today's transitional society, which still considers the elders to be the repositories of the wisdom and history of the people. His house is rarely empty; not only do several grandchildren live there, but sons and sons-in-law keep the shed and meat racks filled, and their wives and children regularly gather there to eat, work, or just visit.

Itu's diminutive wife Ningiu becomes more bent each year as she slowly walks to the stores or to the post office to pick up her Family Allowance cheque or their Old Age pensions. During much of the year Itu works beside the house, building the qamutiks and floe edge boats requested by his sons, other hunters, the Co-op, or some southern museum or collector. Formerly self-confident land people, he and his wife are now equally at ease with such trappings of the consumer society as they choose to adopt; power tools, fridge and freezer, running water, and oil heat. Their voices are well known to Inuit throughout the Arctic, for Itu has recorded marvelous stories of his travels with Canon Turner, the spiritual father of many Anglican Inuit. They have both recorded stories of the old days which are aired by the CBC, and they add their views on current issues to radio phone-in shows.

22 March

A charter arrived from Repulse Bay today, exchanging eighteen people from each settlement. I spent a delightful evening reminiscing with Luki and Adami, who drank tea, gorged themselves on homemade cookies, and fished out the accumulation of rattlers in the centre of my reel table. With a knitting needle, a bent hanger, and much patience and laughter, they recovered several rocks, a spoon, a pencil, a paper clip, a balloon, several bits of paper, and a pop can. They told me that people in Repulse Bay still miss my baked goods.

Any plate of treats is always disposed of to the last crumb before Inuit visitors leave. If the quantity is such that it cannot be eaten immediately, adults and children fill their pockets as they smilingly explain, "for my brother, my Mum, my other children. . . ," so I served no more than I considered reasonable to friends who seemed to have insatiable appetites for home-baked goods. After the people knew me better, they would ask if I had more to sell to them to take home to the rest of the family. Consequently, when my employment with Naujat Co-op was terminated, I approached the Community Council of Repulse Bay for permission to sell baked goods. Soon I was dragging my orange crate to the Community Hall to bingos, dances, movies, and special events.

Inside the large box were stacks of shallow soda pop cartons lined with waxed paper, filled with my wares. Neatly stacked — one lengthwise, the next widthwise — to protect the frozen but fragile contents, the cartons served as removable trays. Tucked into a corner was a small cardboard coffer in which were deployed a sardine tin each for pennies, nickels, dimes, and quarters and a box for bills. Wedged into the remaining space were small empty bags and boxes from dried fruit, bread, drink mix powders, etc. Completing my equipment was a collection of multicoloured, felt-tip-penned price tags: 5¢ for small cookies and krispie squares; 10¢ for large cookies; 15¢ for unfrosted cupcakes; and 20¢ for frosted cupcakes.

Though I towed the whole kit sled fashion, with a blue and white plastic cord, each orange crate withstood many trips across the hard-packed snow from my house to the Community Hall and back. Between sales outings, the orange box remained in my porch, which for almost nine months of the year served as a freezer. The accident that caused me to first sell my wares frozen demonstrated the preferability of hard and firm over crumbly and sticky cakes and frostings. The Inuit thought their frozen state was quite normal and relished the crispness of the cookies, though they were more friable.

It took only one public selling session to direct a stream of customers to my house. At any hour Inuit would drop in for a visit, drink tea, and chat. On the threshold they would turn to inquire, "Do you have any good things for sale?" Groups of youngsters would arrive after school, most with a dime or a quarter to spend, many with younger brothers and sisters clutching a few pennies or a nickel. There was the occasional free spender with a bill. There always seemed to be a plethora of multicoloured, pleated paper circles dotting the snow around my house. Sometimes the twelve-foot by twenty-foot one-room house — ordinarily quite hot when I was baking — would be kept cool by the arrival of wave upon wave of little people, led by their noses and stomachs, come to enjoy a feast of the senses even without money to buy. Some days they were lucky, disposing of broken cookies as well as licking the mixing bowls and egg-beater. Other days they watched, sniffed, and eventually turned to playing with the toys and books in "the children's corner." And sometimes, when the children who had merely come to play in a warm place were quietly donning their mitts and scarves to leave, they would be delighted to choose one cookie or cake each from a proffered plate. The elders — eight- to ten-year-old girls, would hold up an item for the approval of the babies on their backs, all the while keeping an eye on the three- and four-year-olds lest they start grabbing things, shoving them into their pockets and mouths. The rare times when I offered the children a party of juice or tea and treats, they sipped and nibbled in a studied imitation of their parents' visiting behaviour.

The Community Hall opened at least an hour before scheduled events and soon filled with boisterous, active children playing games they improvised using empty pop cans as skates or stilts, brooms for bats and mittens for balls. At my arrival a chorus of "oohs" and "aahs" arose, and a rush of children, reminiscent of a swarm of moths swooping towards a light, scrambled towards the goodie box. There was much pushing and shoving in an effort to see, with the front row almost toppling into my huge box of frozen delicacies as those in back jockeyed for a better position. As the carton-trays filled with cupcakes and layers of cookies and squares were spread over the table, the crowd was thinned by children who went running home for money, and adults left their seats and conversations around the hall to come buy.

It was fun for everyone in those days; the Inuit would buy soft drinks, cigarettes, or candy bars at the canteen, then give the change to the children who would buy something at my cut-rate table. A young shopper would pour out a fistful of change, after due deliberation select an item, then question me with big brown eyes and raised eyebrows, silently yet clearly asking, "More?" At my *"Atii,"* ("Go ahead") the child again bent over the boxes. Brown cake with pink frosting or white cake with no frosting? Oatmeal or peanut butter cookie or krispie square? A four-year-old's purchases might be selected with an eye to sharing with his sister, and when the recipient of this largesse — from her throne in anaana's amauti — threw the cake onto the floor, older brother would pick it up, wipe it off, and coaxingly hand it back to his bright-eyed sibling. Mum never seemed to mind crumbs down her back or frosting in her hair. Eventually the questioning look drew a *"Taima,"* and the pile of purchases was squeezed into an empty cake box or bag and the elated shopper carefully threaded his way through his rambunctious playmates, securely hugging his booty. When a child was knocked down or dropped his precious load, as was bound to happen in the maëlstrom of active youngsters, there were no tears or outbursts. Other children would scramble to pick up the treasures and return them to their owner, often with a wistful look as if hoping the goodies might stick to their hands when the owner tried to take them back. When cookies or krispies met such a fate, there was often only a pile of crumbs left. Sometimes the doleful countenance would soon return to normal as the child ran off to join his peers. At other times the laughing parents would give the child a few more coins to replace the treasure. In either case the child learned that the tragedy of the moment was to be accepted without fuss in the manner his parents had accepted real deprivation in the old days.

When faced with unusual situations — or ingredients — the northern cook reacts with alacrity, substituting and extrapolating with panache. It was of this spirit that "pseudo-jacks" were born.

The Co-op was overstocked — nay, glutted! — with one-pound bags of a nutritious, delicious and unpopular puffed wheat cereal. From $1.87 the bags were marked down to 98¢ and still they gathered dust on the shelves. At 10¢ each I succumbed and repaired to my lair to try puffed wheat squares using my krispies recipe. The soft wheat instead of the brittle rice called for in the recipe, changed the texture and made the squares harder to cut, but they were delicious nonetheless.

Sealift orders, delivered each year before freeze-up, attempt to anticipate the settlement's needs, but each year something is in short supply. That year the extra demand my burgeoning baking business placed on available supplies may have been a factor contributing to the exhaustion of brown sugar stocks barely half way through the supply year. The store managers decided to wait until the annual arctic resupply performance — sealift — rather than bring in the heavy, non-essential item at air freight rates that would double the price. So I fiddled around with the ingredients, cooking temperatures, and amounts and eventually marketed a tasty product using corn syrup and molasses in lieu of brown sugar.

No sooner had my customers developed a taste for the new treat than the village supply of peanut butter was liquidated. No problem ... an additional soupçon of butter, and *voila!* ... the proper consistency with a slight change of flavour.

The butter went next. After the frozen supply was gone, a few cases of tinned butter were found in the back of the warm warehouse, but the contents were so rancid they were sold at a few cents each for dog food. I chose salad oil as a substitute but, unable to bear the stress of yet another mutation, the squares crumbled. But they tasted fine, so I invested in some small, plastic bags and offered what I explained to my customers was "Good — like Cracker Jacks." When the vanilla ran out and I switched to almond extract, the two teaspoons of salt were all that remained of the original recipe. After weeding out the correct ingredients, amounts, and instructions, I discarded the sticky recipe file card in favour of a neatly typed, fresh card entitled — logically enough, "pseudo-jacks."

Near the end of that school year at Repulse Bay I was invited to join the girls on a fishing-through-the-ice picnic. On the appointed day the picnic was cancelled because a storm was blowing in from the south. I tossed my peanut butter and jelly and cheese sandwiches into my freezer box and forgot them until I towed my crate to a movie a few nights later. As I was arranging my wares at the Community Hall, a scuffle developed, out of which came cries of "How much? How much?" A couple of the older boys had pounced on the sandwiches from my erstwhile lunch and were hungrily demanding a price for them.

"That's my lunch! It's not for sale."

"Why not?" came the answer.

"Indeed, why not?" I thought, and thus — more or less by popular demand — another sale item was launched. When I complained to friends that I found baking bread for the sandwiches too time-consuming, they begged me not to stop selling them but to switch to bakery bread. Next several Inuit offered to furnish caribou meat if I would cook it and make meat sandwiches for them to buy, but about then I moved to Igloolik.

After some time in my new home I approached the Igloolik Settlement Council for a business license, relieved the Co-op of their unmarketable stock of angel food cake mix at a discount, put in a sealift order for sugars, flour, and margarine, and, during the winter, started having "bake sales" at my house. Pseudo-jacks were as popular as they had been at Repulse Bay, and the cookie varieties expanded to include fascinating flavours — originated to use cases of pie filling given me by friends when they were transferred south. The same pattern as had developed in the smaller settlement developed in Igloolik, though I had fewer adult customers except on days of an announced sale. Then men would buy whole trays of treats, somehow balancing them as they roared off on their snow machines. The usual trade was children with bright eyes, sweet teeth, and a few coins, who furnished a welcome diversion from my writing. By a happy coincidence, I determined to spend my time — and earn my money — in other pursuits at the same time that the Housing Association suggested that businesses should not be conducted in government-subsidized, low-rental units.

I still make cupcakes, cookies, and pseudo-jacks to distribute to friends and neighbours, some of whom always make sure I have enough country food. I've always been satisfied with the water delivery service in Igloolik; is it because I never fail to fill the hands of the water men with whatever baked goods I have on hand if I'm home when they deliver?

Last Hallowe'en I invited each group of goblins in so that I could admire their costumes as I put handfuls of pseudo-jacks into their goodie bags. "That little rascal's been here before," I thought when one bunch was leaving. Then in came another familiar costume! During the next few days I heard that quite a few of the appreciative little scamps had come several times before I caught on to their game!

23 March

It *is* spring, though Itu tells me it is only the "season-before-spring," spring being the season when there are puddles on the ice, and right now the snow is just evaporating. Yesterday I saw a black smudge on the top of the forty-five-gallon fuel drum in front of my house, and today the bottom of the frying pan that spent the winter there is plainly visible. In the bright morning sun I shovelled the snow off the roof over the windows, to cut to a minimum the spring-time river that appears on the floor underneath them. In two days, with the help of the vacuum cleaner blowing, the huge cake of ice between my window panes has been melted, and I can enjoy the light. It is light by 4:00 A.M. now, a fact I ordinarily would not know, but a neighbour was drinking the other night, and his wife took refuge with me at 3:00 A.M. We watched the sky pinken until by four o'clock it was light. Later a bright, white streak on the snow caught my eye. It was a shaft of light reflected from a ragged face on a chunk of drinking water ice in the snow in front of Itu's house.

24 March

"A Chinese wants to buy frozen polar bears?" I asked incredulously.

"Stand up!" Toby commanded. When he tried to show me what the purchaser wanted I leaped back and hit the sugar spoon. While Sila mopped sugar off her face and neck, Toby left me in peace — and ignorance. This morning the game officer enlightened me.

At the Hunters' and Trappers' Association meeting last night, they studied a letter from an Oriental offering a good price for frozen polar bear gall bladders. The qallunaaq had explained to the puzzled Inuit that the gall bladders, and also caribou antlers, are made into youth potions and aphrodisiacs. Any scheme for earning money receives serious consideration from people eager to enjoy the increasing number of novelties available not only in the Hudson's Bay store, but also in their own Co-operative. Hunters who sold six- and eight-foot polar bear pelts for $5 in the 1930s know that today they may receive over $100 a foot for a prime skin. Wives who once sewed polar-bear-skin clothing for their men now only do so if the skin is unmarketable, and they may even sell polar-bear-skin mitts, stockings, or pants for cash. However, after considering the logistical difficulties involved in delivering the organs frozen, the men reluctantly abandoned the idea of selling polar bear gall bladders.

The next item on the agenda — the newly initiated government policy of buying polar bear skulls and genitals — caused the Inuit to ask if the Canadian government was going into the business of making love potions.

27 March — Wednesday in Holy Week

With clear weather there was a Saturday exodus to the floe edge and lots of meat is in evidence today. Behind Inaq's house a baby ujjuk — frozen solid — is stuck upright in the snow.

The students arrived from Frobisher Bay on last night's plane, but word has come that the high school students in Ottawa and trade apprentices in Winnipeg will not be sent home for Easter at government expense.

The furnace was lit several days ago to warm up the stone church. During the long Easter services I shall wear caribou-skin stockings in my kamiks, and sheepskin overshoes, in hopes that this year my poor, immobile feet will not speak to me louder than the beautiful liturgy of the season. Aesthetically I love that church, but my feet hate it.

The Holy Week services, which start tomorrow with commemoration of the Last Supper and Catholic First Communion in the stone church, were announced over the radio this noon, followed by a string of requests for parka fur and duffel, then some hunters made arrangements to go bring in high walrus from last fall's caches. It's hard to remember this community without CBII-fm, Igloolik Community Radio. It serves the combined functions of bulletin board, newspaper, theatre, telephone, companion, teacher, jester, pastor, judge, and jury. I miss the atmosphere of meetings when people gathered to hear committee candidates speak, or the forum assembled to debate current interests amid the wails and googlings of the babies, the air heavy with smoke and diapers, laughter, and camaraderie. Those gatherings were ideal for the children to play and the young people to flirt, but not so good for old people to voice their opinions, something they can now do merely by lifting the phone. Instead of one large group debating, there are now small groups around tea pots in various houses, listening to the radio, discussing, and sometimes phoning in. Campaign speeches are pre-recorded and aired when convenient. As often as not they are interrupted several times to ask a child to phone home, invite anyone interested to partake of boiled caribou, igunaq, or some other delicacy, or to announce the title of the evening's movie at the Community Hall.

Last night a French film crew arrived to capture the simple magic of an Inuit Easter for the delectation of European TV audiences. I find myself on the defensive towards film crews, photographers, anthropologists, and such delvers into the thoughts and ways of others. Some of the sincere, competent researchers who have passed through the Transient Centre have made me aware of my biased narrowness in contrast to their accepting professionalism. But I have also been surfeited with photographers intent on picturing dog teams and round, smiling Inuit faces framed in fur. These do still exist in Igloolik but are almost obscured by snow machines of all makes and the fur is most apt to be on store-bought down parkas.

Four people are to leave on Friday's flight to join those from Arctic Bay chartering a DC-3 to Thule Qänaq to spend the Easter weekend in Greenland. In 1969, Fr. Mary-Rousselière organized — with State Department aid — the first Inuit foreign charter. Now native members of the Inuit Language Commission, Inuit Circumpolar Conference, and other organizations travel between Alaska, Canada, and Greenland without a second thought.

After the redistribution of ridings to expand elected representation in the Legislative Assembly of the Northwest Territories, all the settlements left over from natural divisions in the eastern Arctic were tossed into Foxe Basin riding. Repulse Bay and Coral Harbour are reached from Winnipeg through Churchill, Manitoba; and Hall Beach, Igloolik, and Cape Dorset through Frobisher Bay from Montreal. But for the elected representative, Mark Evaluardjuk, to reach Cape Dorset from his home, Igloolik, he had to fly to Frobisher Bay then wait several days for a plane to Cape Dorset. Instead of going through Montreal, Winnipeg, and Churchill to visit Repulse Bay, he would charter a Twin Otter for the hour-and-fifteen-minute flight from Hall Beach, then continue on the forty-five minutes to Coral Harbour. I was one of many people delighted to pay a small fare to visit in Repulse Bay thus helping to defray the cost of the aircraft. The riding has now been more reasonably redrawn, but the taste for low-fare, charter travel has persisted, and each year there are more Twin Otters hired to carry relatives and friends between Pond Inlet, Arctic Bay, Repulse Bay, and Igloolik.

April

8 April

Monday, and school starts again after the week of Easter festivities. Somehow I managed to drag myself out of bed this morning to go fix breakfast at the Transient Centre without the past week's incentive of a dance before work. One dance lasted until 10:00 A.M., though most ended before 8:00 A.M., and once when I went by at 6:30, the hall was already quiet.

Uinga and Jeannie have come in with a group from Agu Bay to bring her widowed mother Piqak and adopted younger brother Joshua, who have been given a house behind mine. Uinga was maintenance man for the Nursing Station, a member of several committees, a radio announcer, and Chairman of the Board of Directors of the Co-op when he announced last spring that he was going to give up his house and job to take advantage of the Northwest Territories Government Outpost Camp Assistance Program to go and live at Agu Bay. His wife Jeannie — who speaks excellent English — told me she was not only looking forward to performing the traditional woman's jobs but also to accompanying her husband hunting. "People criticize me because I like to go hunting. When I leave the girls with my mum and go to the floe edge, some of the women say it is not right, that a woman should not go out hunting alone or that a mother should take her children with her. I don't think that way," she laughed, "so I don't act that way!"

The Agu Bay people arrived just as the stone church emptied on the evening of Holy Thursday. A knot of Inuit formed along the shore to meet the two qamutiks pulled by ten dogs each. Among the group on the beach, Jeannie's warmly dressed family bore witness to her flair, in the original cut of nine-year-old Louise's new parka cover, the extraordinary design on her husband's garment, and little Jolly's stylish tuque and mittens.

The men helped unload the sleds while the women, babies on their backs, hands pushed up the sleeves of their amautis, stood rocking from one foot to the other, happily chatting amongst themselves. The newcomers were welcomed with silent grins and the limp handshakes that are barely a touching of hands. Even the babies were included in this warm but silent greeting, as the women bent forward, twisting their pouches so that the babies could share a smile and touch of the hand. The Inuit had no word of greeting until recently, when some were coined at the insistence of visitors from other cultures, and they still do not babble when they meet again after a long separation. Later, over tea or meat, little by little, questions are exchanged, news and stories of trips related, and conversation flourishes.

At 9:00 P.M. the Easter moon hung wanly in a pale blue sky, that shaded to soft pink and lavender close to the land and sea. There was a ridge of smokey blue cloud along the horizon, marking the open water of the floe edge, and the sun shone from behind the village, lighting up the chunks of pack ice on the bay and tossing shadows out behind them. Easter was early this year so it was dark for the Vigil Service but dawning at 2:30 A.M. when we started home after the tea and biscuits gathering in the mission. The religious observance of Easter Week starts with the Vigil Service in the stone church at midnight. Around five hundred of the village's seven hundred and ninety Anglicans and Catholics crowd into the building. The Inuit wear the new kamiks whose ujjuk soles women have been chewing as they went about the hamlet during past weeks, and everyone wears some new, colourfully embroidered piece of clothing.

Liturgy in Igloolik is always action-packed, however, the parishioners tend to vie with the officiants to produce more action in the pews than in the sanctuary. Toddlers recover dropped and thrown bottles for little ones in amautis while others stretch or climb up onto benches to rub noses with their tiny friends on mother's back. Now and then a woman will climb out of a row to carry a sleeping child across the aisle to father, who gently beds it down on the floor under the benches. There is more room on the men's side since the great majority of waddlers and crawlers play on the women's side close to breast and bottle. Towards the end of the service I got the impression that two sound-tracks were being played simultaneously: there was the hymn, with the women calmly singing one verse and the men the next, and there was the screaming, squealing, cooing, and crying of the babies.

The eleven o'clock Easter morning services in both the Anglican and the Roman Catholic churches were much quieter, for the noisemakers of the Vigil Service were at home sound asleep. However, they were all up and dressed for the start of the games at the Roman Catholic mission, which lasted all afternoon until evening prayer services. During the weeks following Christmas and Easter every year the people improvise all kinds of games but each season always starts with nugluktaq — thread-the-spear. A vertebra or a piece of ivory with a hole carved in it is hung from the ceiling just as it used to be hung from the dome of the iglu. Players, each with a pointed stick or spear, encircle the dangling target, and, at the command, all try to be the first to impale it. Players are grouped according to sex and size and may use only one hand, but there seem to be no other rules. Since people have started bringing their own long, pointed sticks instead of using a piece of bone or ivory, the furious pecking can result in bloodied hands, but the protagonists just laugh and howl all the louder, and remember to wear a glove on their playing hand during the next bout. There was also "dancing" at the mission. Neither Inuktitut square dances nor rock teen dances, these are a variation of musical chairs using humans instead of chairs, and are played with unbelievable gusto.

The routine for the week was; sleep in the morning, outdoor games on the ice or snow in the afternoons, and games and dances at the Community Hall all night. This year the sea ice in front of the village provided an ideal terrain for foot, dog team, snowmobile, and novelty races such as three-legged and gunny-sack.

Every year there are fewer dog teams and more motor toboggans. The motor races are never just for speed and are seldom twice the same. In one race this year, drivers had to balance empty ten-gallon fuel drums on their shoulders while covering the course. In another, men, then women, towed a pop can secured to their machines by a strand of thread, often stopping to retie the broken tow line. On Tuesday a man gave me a ride (wilder than the race!) out to the turn-around marker on the end of the island during a race of snow-machines towing qamutiks with unsecured forty-five gallon drums on them. One contestant came around the cairn standing tall in the saddle, shouting commands to his ski-doo as it if were his team of dogs.

One dog team race was for men over sixty with their wives on the qamutik. Siaku, a helper at the Hudson's Bay store, has long been a widower and has no dogs. He was loaned a team and Itu's wife for the occasion and caused roars of laughter and salacious remarks when his team took off across the island instead of along the sea ice course followed by the other teams. There was also a race for qallunaat. The competence of this select group ranged from the excellent of the teacher, who has raised his own team, through the credible performance of some other "old northern hands," to the hilarious mêlée of dogs, drivers, qamutiks, and children when several teams (including mine) bolted for their stake-out areas.

After one-, two-, and three-dog races with tiny qamutiks for the children, the organizers commandeered the little sleds for an old ladies' special. Each woman crouched as best she could on the conveyance and was pulled by one man. The women were giggling so hard they kept rolling off before the race even started. The same ladies elicited much laughter by their efforts to guide their teams of three blindfolded human "dogs" using only the customary "*ouay,*" *aiye,*" and "*wah*" commands.

From my window I can see the remains of some of the festivities . . . the snow-block wind shelter in which several people made tea on camp stoves, the toppling Towers of Babel stacked by competitors for the prize of a "snow knife" — a thin- bladed butcher knife, and the snow-wall backdrop for an RCMP-sponsored rifle shoot, now a slide for the children. I think the second-prize winner in the rifle shoot did his practising in penny arcades in Ottawa, though the winner was a "real" hunter, and Pita won the "lucky spot" prize of a .22 rifle, having hit a pre-marked, random spot on the target. Other games and prizes were sponsored by the Bay, the Co-op, the Parish Council and Vestry Committee, Radio Society, Hunters' and Trappers' Association, Hamlet Council, Recreation Committee. . . in short, every organization in town.

There were whip-cracking, ice-chiseling, and harpoon-throwing jousts on the sea ice and various iglu-building contests have left play areas for the children in snowbanks all around the settlement. The weather was so good this year that each day there was another snow-house-building contest: for right-handed men using their left hands and for left-handed men using their right hands; for men using a snow knife only instead of the customary saw and knife; for women; for couples; for women pairs. One set of contestants was asked to finish all the structures. Later each house was claimed by a woman who demonstrated, rather than competed in, making tea as it was done in the old days, starting with pounding the animal fat to make oil for the stone lamps used to boil the water. The process took the entire afternoon and people brought caribou skins and sat on the snow in the sun chatting while the French TV crew alternated between euphoria with the scene and despair with their freezing fingers and film.

Games were even interjected in the dancing every evening. There was a fishing party for women over sixty, of whom there were six. They stood on two benches facing each other, each with a thread tied to a bent-pin hook. With this they had to catch the loops of thread tying folded pieces of paper on the floor between the benches. As each woman pulled up a paper, its nonsense verse was read aloud before the woman was awarded the prize hinted at in the lines. Piqak was presented with a bright blouse "to wear on your next trip to Montreal or to summer camp to skin seals." Among the feats-of-strength competitions for all ages of men and women were two-person tugs-of-war using an ujjuk thong stretched between two bones; a match in which contestants sitting back on their heels on the floor, jumped to their feet, the winner being the one who succeeded the most times; and what I always think of as the Cossack dance for men, women, and children.

It is impossible to observe all the activities going on, for people wander back and forth between the ice and the Community Hall, warming up with tea or boiled meat, or visiting with neighbours and friends in town for the season. Sometimes, for games like the men-over-sixty dog-team race and the ladies' fishing expedition runners have to be sent to round up participants.

Recent soft snow has piled into tide cracks and drifted around ice blocks pushed up along the shore by winter tides. One day I saw two boys on a small qamutik pulled by two confused dogs, making slow progress from the game sites beyond the pressure ice. They yawed this way and that, both dogs floundering in soft snow up to their bellies. More than once, dog or sled or both sank into the drifts around ice blocks and cracks. The equipage paraded around on the sea ice spreading a ripple of havoc wherever it went. The dogs would materialize next to someone who would move out of the way, only to find the dogs moving in the same direction. A group would see them coming, try to determine which way to flee, guess wrong, and end up straddling the tow lines. At other times people would disperse, leaving a clear lane for the animals which would promptly sit down. They won Best of Show hands down . . . or paws up!

The snow buntings — first harbingers of spring — arrived sometime during the festivities.

The people who visited Greenland returned on Friday, but a sad note was the departure of Inaq's wife Alitsiaq as a med evac. She has had a recurrence of TB bad enough to send her once again to Montreal General Hospital coughing and spitting blood.

This afternoon after lunch I noticed people spread all over the ice, just walking around slowly. Pita explained to me, grinning, that he had hidden a wall clock somewhere on the ice and whoever found it could keep it. Government offices in Frobisher Bay and Yellowknife chafe because their phone calls are not answered during Easter Week. I wonder what they're saying today. . . .

10 April

Pita came by pulling a qamutik and when I waved, he slowed down, allowing me to flop onto the sled beside Ikpunu who welcomed me with a grin, squeezed my thigh, and announced, "I would like to sleep with you." I took it as a joke, knowing he meant it, and at the store prowled around behind counters trying to avoid him. Every time I popped out he was there smiling with such ardent looks that I was embarassed. Thoroughly rattled, I gave up shopping, chatted with the cashiers for a moment, and made my getaway.

One façet of Inuit promiscuity that amazes me is that a man or woman with a steady girlfriend or boyfriend "on the side" nevertheless loves his or her partner and family. The missionaries note that the family was so important in the camp days that nothing was allowed to destroy it. Add an Inuk's view of sex as a delightful indoor sport unrelated to the romantic ideas of many cultures, and you come up with the prevailing openness concerning extramarital exploits and relationships, and episodes like today's. Ikpunu's wife has a boyfriend and has more than once tried to fix me up with her husband. I have a knack of falling into these situations, finding out too late that some-one was looking for a sexual partner when the invitation was issued for the weekend on the land or the hunt which I am innocently enjoying.

30

What I also find charming — and reassuring! — is that the gentlemen accept a laughing "no thanks" and cup of tea with a shrug and a grin. I've met no Lotharios among the older men, but the young bilingual Inuit, sometimes high, adopt a more qallunaak attitude, becoming offended or querulous. Once, when I was discussing their attitude towards sex with one of my bilingual Inuit friends, she offered to get me a man any time I wanted one. I was so surprised I don't know what I said, but she went on to explain that it would be quite all right as long as the wife approved and the man was in my age bracket. I thanked her and joked that I'm qallunaak enough that, if I did want a man, part of the fun would be getting him. Even now, after living here for so many years, I still receive indiscreet invitations, and I think my morale would sink without the booster of a proposition now and then. Cindy, a qallunaaq from Vancouver, is delightful in her indignant rebuffals of young swains who visit when her Inuk husband is out on his trapline or hunting. She fits well into the society of her in-laws, except for the promiscuity, against which she waxes indignant.

Iglus are blossoming around town. One lad has built a bedroom behind his dad's house where he and his lady may awake and turn on the pink-and-blue teddy-bear lamp whose cord is strung from the house. An electric lamp also illuminates the caribou skins, camp stove, and sewing supplies in the snow house in front of Siaku's, and the carving and sewing workshop iglu up on the hill by the hamlet garage appears larger as the snowbanks around it evaporate. And I was not assigned one of the rehabilitated houses. Already I have my eye on one to be done next year, with bedroom windows facing west, which I would prefer to the east-windowed house I didn't get this year.

11 April

There is lots of activity early in the mornings now that the sun is high, the weather beautiful, and the mercury at $-25°C$ to $0°$. On a roof in the distance someone is shovelling off the soft, wet snow that fell last night. "Night" is a euphemism for the coloured glow that now envelops only the midnight hours. The other night, as I went to the Community Hall around 11:30, it was thinly dark with the last rose-to-lavender glow in the north-west. When I came home at 2:30 A.M., the sunrise had moved the pink over slightly to the east on the northern horizon and touched up the mauve to a soft rose.

Atani is hitching up his dogs to go to Tunit's outpost camp at Ikpikitturjuaq. They are wild with joy, howling and performing their own happy dance step, bouncing on firmly planted hind legs, with stiff front legs. They look like woolly rocking horses. As Atani works on one dog the others express their excitement by running and jousting for the short distance their tethers allow. They bob around each other in circles, fluffy tails curling and uncurling. The whole chain of dogs is an animated, vociferous mass quite different from the silent line of snow-encrusted mounds the team so often presents.

This morning I witnessed a northern rodeo act. Three men on snowmachines were rounding up an errant dog team. One man would herd five or six dogs together and get them running in the right direction, then the pack would break, half going one way and half the other. One driver corralled two dogs and drove off at a good clip. One dog managed to stay on his feet, but the other raised a white plume of soft snow as he was dragged along. From time to time the driver glanced back but he slowed down nary a whit. Another driver, of a more tender disposition, drove slowly enough for the two dogs following him to keep their footing. The third machine came careening over the ice with a dog slung, sack-like, across the lap of the driver.

On the way to the Co-op I stopped to chat with Itu as he worked on yet another qamutik. Five of varying ages are lying around the house. When I remarked on the seal skin and dog skin hanging on the clothes line, he grinned and grabbed the dog skin saying, "Here. Make yourself a nose-warmer!" He asked if I need meat which I do not, since I just bargained with Levi to do his income tax in exchange for some caribou. Itu pretended to scold me "Ask for meat when you need it. Do not go without, waiting for someone to give it to you."

Suzie and her eighth-grade chum, Sally, helped carry my groceries home from the Co-op. Suzie tells me her dad (Toby) was assigned one of the new four-bedroom houses at the Housing Association meeting last night. I'm glad for them but sad for me. They are good neighbours and I will miss watching Natika and Tommy in their caribou-skin clothing getting ready to go hunting early in the morning when I go to fix breakfast at the Transient Centre. Sometimes, if I stop on my way back from cooking lunch, they are already home, and Sila will have a pile of seal skins to scrape.

The girls were poring over old photos taken the spring I went camping at Situqarvik with Vira and her family. "What are you doing back there?" asked Suzie. It was the picture of me seated on the rocks behind Nulia, diligently scraping a seal skin. "You scraped a seal skin?" Sally cried incredulously. "It was an old scarred, brown skin that no one wanted," I explained, "so Uqangi let me have it." Then I told the girls how eight-year-old Theresa and I had gone to skin the seal where the hunter told us he had left it, and how we had done well until we got to the tail. Neither of us could remember what the tail looks like on a prepared skin. But we managed. The entire following day I sat in the sun next to Nulia, hacking away with my ulu, removing the fat from my yellow and brown pelt while Nulia deftly flensed her silky silver and black patterned skins. Every few minutes she would sharpen her ulu with lightning strokes against a small hunting knife, smile, and put a new edge on my instrument for me. When my arm felt limp and my fingers cramped around the ulu knife, I would tuck the pelt into a puddle in a rock and rest, but Nulia never slackened her pace. At the end of the day I laid out my finished skin on the rocks among Nulia's six. I was dismayed when I saw that, even from a distance, the brown skin looked lumpy, so I put it in a puddle for the night and spent two more days redoing it, after which Vira and I started to sew up the many places I had cut it. Fortunately, just then Uqangi decided it was time to return to Repulse Bay, and I had a legitimate excuse to abandon the piece of brown sealskin lace.

"That looks like Sara," Sally pointed to a woman in a tent full of people.

"You're right," I answered as Suzie exclaimed, "Look how young Tukilaq looks," then turned the page and added, "There's his mum Siuti with teeth!" Siuti had been my first "mother" in Repulse Bay, trying to teach me the language, helping me chew my sealskin kamiks to fit, and making me welcome in her home and camp. Her husband, Oqak, was a descendant of George Washington Cleveland, the Repulse Bay trader mentioned in the writings of several explorers and anthropologists. Though one of the tallest men in the village, Oqak was of slight build. He had a long, narrow face, prominent nose, slightly wavy, wispy hair, and bright blue eyes. However, it was not his appearance people commented on when his name was mentioned, but his loquaciousness. I had been able to catch what he was saying long before I had learned enough Inuktitut to understand anyone else because he expressed himself not only with his voice, but with every muscle of his body. Face working, hands fluttering, arms flailing, body twisting, he could talk for hours without respite. Among a people reknowned for storytelling, Oqak was legendary.

The first time I ever went seal hunting was with Oqak and his eldest son Tukilaq, even taller than he. The hunters had killed several small white beluga whales near the settlement that morning. When Oqak and Tukilaq returned for more ammunition, I had been allowed to go back out hunting with them. All day Oqak kept up a running commentary from his seat at the stern by the outboard motor. When he fired at a seal and missed, he would inspect his rifle, gesticulate wildly, tracing the curved flight of the trajectory with his arm and shaking the faulty weapon before tossing it into the bottom of the boat, only to start the whole performance over again the next time he missed a shot. Throughout the day Tukilaq sat quietly, smiling at his father's antics, firing only when the older man told him to do so. Sometimes, if Tukilaq's bullet hit its mark, his father would threaten to trade his defective rifle for the good one of his son. Tukilaq would silently hook the animal, pull it into the canoe, and drape the head over the side until the seal stopped bleeding. But when Oqak made a kill, he became even more voluble.

By the end of the day, when we started home with seven seals, I was weak from laughing. My reputation as a talisman probably dates from that day, for we cut quite a figure putting up to the shore. On the way home we picked up three whales killed that morning and tied to floats. We towed two whales on one side and one on the other side of the canoe, and two seals were draped over the bow. The bottom of the canoe was covered with gear and seals, two of which served as glossy, plump pillows for Tukilaq and me, sitting very still to prevent the overfull vessel from shipping water.

Suzie and Sally laughed at my tale, for they recognized the hunters well from my description. Tukilaq, his wife Sara, and their children had moved to Igloolik before me, joining his two sisters, married to Igloolik men. Oqak and Siuti came fairly often to visit, spending a few weeks in Igloolik before going on to visit friends and relatives in Arctic Bay, Nanisivik, and Hall Beach as well as outpost camps at Ikpikitturjuak and Agu Bay.

12 April

It is one of those lovely days when the master of the elements either cannot make up his mind or decides to empty his bag of weathers.

Clouds scud across a pale blue sky one minute, casting shadows in the bright sun. The next minute fine snow swirls in sheets onto the settlement and through the crack in my toilet, allowing a fine mist to drift down onto the seat. It is blowing hard but seems warm, though my thermometer reads −20°C.

In the street, a pack of children ranging from staggering babies to young teen-agers puff clouds of vapour into the spring air as they scramble after a ball.

In the sun streaming through the window at Toby's house, he and Angut face each other across the table, sipping tea while discussing the details of the hunt that has netted them six seals. Sitting on the floor, one foot tucked under her, the other leg outstretched, is Angut's wife Arnak facing the squatting Sila. Between the women lies a metal platter about sixteen inches in diameter, heaped with neat piles of raw seal liver, white seal fat dappled on one side with red, and dark red, almost black, chunks of seal meat. A butcher knife lies ignored on the platter as the women attack the food with short, expert swipes of their round-bladed ulus.

The hostess, holding her bloody hands well away from her clothing, repairs to the furnace room, returning to place a brimming gaily patterned enamel bowl on the floor next to the platter. Her visitor's raised eyebrows add force to her smile as the next course is contemplated: raw bearded seal intestines. While Arnak daintily severs the membrane around the large intestine and slices off a layer of muscle without puncturing the organ, her hostess first squeezes a length of small intestine through her fingers, then draws the same length through her clenched teeth. Finally she grasps a piece of the loosened membrane between her teeth and peels away a portion, which she bites off and chews with relish. There is little conversation around the platter and bowl as the two women enjoy a rare, leisurely meal without the interruptions of children.

22 April, Repulse Bay

Jenny Richardson, photographer and writer, has hired Atani to bring her to Repulse Bay by dog team and he says that I may return to Igloolik with him! They left several days ago and I fear the warmth will do me out of the return trip.

I came to Repulse Bay with Oqak, his wife Siuti, their little adopted son, and my teen-age friends, Luki, whose sister is married to

Oqak's son Nukinaq, and Luki's school chum, Adami. It was about twenty below when we left Igloolik, rising to almost zero with more and more ragged patches in the snow cover as we neared Repulse Bay. During the four days we have been here, the temperature has even been above freezing and as it rises my hopes of returning by dog team sink. Atani is expected from one day to the next, but I'm sure he'll want to visit at least a week once he gets here and by then the season will be too far advanced for the slow trip home. I suspect he will leave his dogs and qamutik here, fly back to Igloolik, and either come get them or have someone bring them to him when it is again possible to travel across the snow and ice between the two settlements.

On Friday afternoon the twelfth of April, our party left Igloolik on two qamutiks with Tukilaq and a family from Hall Beach right behind us. While we frolicked in the snow we could see our travelling companions in the distance going straight through to Hall Beach, which they reached in three hours. Due to our reduced speed and long tea and play break, our travel time was five hours. We stayed at Hall Beach three sleeps, and when we finally set out Jamesi and his wife Kati were travelling with us.

We stopped at a cabin, vacated by a family which, in 1975, was the last one to move into Hall Beach from the old camps. From the outside it looked like a large, rough cube of snow. A snow-block tunnel led to a door into the one small room. It was papered with magazine pages, and in the wastebasket was a 1974 issue of *Fortune* magazine. Siuti and Kati examined everything minutely. Hanging above a shelf were a blue plastic flashlight and a caribou antler scraper or ladle. On the shelf lay a frozen chicken in its Cry-O-Vac wrapper. The women carefully replaced each item, including two Polaroid photographs taken on the nearby beach during the summer. In the iglu that night Oqak produced a girlie magazine — presumably from the cabin and no doubt compliments of the DEW line — and gave us a running commentary of page after page of nudes.

To my mind, one of the luxuries of iglu travel is the sleep of exhaustion. Several times on this trip as on others, I found myself so tired when building the iglu that I had to concentrate on making the muscles function, only managing through specific acts of the will. I have felt as if my heart would stop beating if I did not command it to continue. But once the snow block is pushed into the opening for the night, time ceases while body and soul are rejuvenated during evenings of feasting, games, and storytelling. Nor is the relaxed atmosphere dispelled by rude awakenings. Each morning of this trip Oqak talked, smoked, made and drank tea, served us and urged us to serve ourselves for literally hours while we napped, put on one sock, and drowsily pondered the merits of donning the other. Though Oqak started the ripple of action around 5:00 A.M., it was usually 10:00 before it had swelled enough to empty the iglu, load the sleds, and drink the last tea before rolling on our way.

Most travellers make the trip from Hall Beach to Repulse Bay in two sleeps while the young bloods drive straight through. We slept four nights. This was my first long trip behind a machine instead of dogs and I was thankful for Oqak's relaxed pace that allowed would-be travelling companions to catch up with us and pass on. Even so, it was only by making sure my duffel bag was strapped soft-side-up, and endeavouring always to land on it, that the thumping and banging of the long sled didn't inflict permanent damage on my flopping body.

Jamesi and Kati spent the first night with us then went on ahead, arriving in Repulse Bay several days before us. Next Simagak, his wife Dora, and two of their children joined us for a day and night and also went on ahead. Tea breaks were always leisurely affairs, and the day Simagak's family was with us Siuti cut a large block of snow with a snow knife and carved a polar bear. The little ones played with the snow bear until it crumbled under the onslaught of the six- and eight-year-old hunters stalking it and using it for target practice. When the children tired of trying to fashion another bear, they built a child-sized, lopsided iglu.

Before they left us to hurry on to Repulse Bay, Simagak shot a caribou which turned out to be a pregnant female. The foetus, about eighteen inches long, was a beautiful miniature which exuded a very strong odour, unexpectedly sweet and spicy.

I usually travelled with Luki and Adami, though sometimes one of the boys drove Oqak's machine while he rode on the qamutik with his wife and child. The third day out there were patches of bare rock and tundra and the pungency of heather crushed by the racing vehicles provided a welcome change from the exhaust fumes of previous days. Once Siuti gathered some of the heather and made smoke to scent our tea. Oqak scoffed, but I enjoyed the brew. That was also the day I kept asking myself which I preferred — snow-blindness or a frozen nose — as I alternately removed my frost-covered glasses and pulled my scarf over my nose, then put the glasses back on and let my nose go unscarfed.

Another one of Oqak's sons, Nukinaq, joined us in our fourth iglu. After an evening of visiting, when the rest of us had bedded down, Luki and Adami set off for Repulse Bay, leaving Nukinaq to be my personal chauffeur for the last lap of the trip.

Nukinaq vied with Oqak for the jester's scepter. When he could no longer tolerate the leisurely pace required to stay behind the party chief, he would slowly draw ahead, exploding into an exuberant burst of speed once the others were out of sight. His high-spirited spurts translated into bouncing contortions for me, hanging on as best I could as the careening qamutik sailed off barely perceptible bumps or hillocks to come slapping down with a force that made me marvel at the durability of the Inuit qamutik . . . and of the people who rode them. Then, as the motor revolutions became slower and slower, his entire body would wilt and slump until — as the engine died — he would flop back onto the snowmachine seat, limp arms dangling to the sides. In a moment he would jump up, turn to me, grinning, and busy himself making tea, which the rest of the party would gladly share when they caught up with us.

Unfortunately, we were in our proper place — behind Oqak — when we ran out of gas. Since all the fuel was on the other sled, we had no alternative but to wait until we were missed. I stepped onto the ice, and Nukinaq immediately appropriated my perch on the qamutik, settling down for a nap. I climbed among the fairyland forms of pack and pressure ice along the shore, so absorbed in exploring the ice jungle that before I even noticed his arrival Oqak was lashing down his load, eager to be gone.

One of our stops that last day was at the site of the famous bear episode that cinched my Repulse Bay reputation as a good luck omen and dispelled much of the hunters' reluctance to let me accompany them. Oqak, Nukinaq, and I had set out one bright November day to check their net under the ice of a nearby lake. On the trail we met Tukilaq, Oqak's oldest son, who had left a haunch of caribou rolled in the skin by the fish net and was returning to the settlement. For all their trouble, the men had taken only two fish. They were replacing the net when Jamesi drove up with Oqak's youngest son, Malak, on his qamutik. They had shot and wounded a polar bear with two yearling cubs. The bears had swum to an island. We drove the few miles to the shore facing the island and built an iglu. Since none of us had planned on being out overnight, we had no sleeping skins or bags, only the single caribou pelt strapped to each qamutik. We were grateful not only for the caribou meat Tukilaq had left us, but also for the extra skin. Oqak stuck a piece of tightly twisted paper bag into a block of margarine, making a candle by whose light we drank tea, finished off the pilot biscuits and fish, and ate our fill of fresh, frozen caribou.

We spent the night fully dressed, huddled together on the three caribou skins with nothing to put over us. It seemed as if every time I drifted into a fitful sleep, Oqak would announce "It's cold!" in stentorian tones, and with such a lugubrious air that we could not help but laugh. His dissertations on the depth, texture, density, and other assorted attributes of the cold, given while he caulked wind-leaking cracks between the snow blocks, helped pass the night. In the morning the inside of the structure was decorated with a strip of boldly patterned cotton artfully draped from several holes, and the knotted remains of a mitten and torn bits of paper bag stuffed into other holes around the white dome.

It was barely dawn when we set out for the island. Close to shore we threaded our way among towering blocks of stranded ice. Out farther the chunks were floating, covered with the opaque white new ice which also bent under foot but sometimes crumpled around the jagged edges of tilted ice cakes. Oqak led the single file while I brought up the rear, engrossed in the game of scaling the slippery sides of canted ice, pulling a foot up quickly before it sank all the way through the elastic new ice into the water below and enjoying the leader's antics. Once I held my breath as he disappeared in a white whoosh behind an upended block. We all laughed at his comical expression as he peeked around the side of the treacherous obstacle a moment later. When he dropped to his hands and knees to spread out his weight and reduce the number of times he broke through the rolling layer of white mush, we followed his example. A few yards later he turned and motioned for me to go back. When the four men had finally convinced me that I had correctly understood the command, I turned my back on them and my stomach drew into a knot. I faced what seemed like an interminable expanse of threatening, jagged ice that I must cross all alone! Soon I was once again concentrating so hard on each step that no other thought or emotion disturbed me. Later, the men explained, "We sent you back because the tide was not out far enough. It was dangerous."

At the island the men had found the dead mother bear. One cub lay with its head on its mother's neck crying and snarling and lunging at whoever tried to approach. The other cub they lassoed and secured to a large boulder where he growled and chewed at the restraining rope while the men examined their predicament.

"In the old days we would have killed the cubs because they cannot survive without their mother. Now the government tells us a bear must be a certain size before we kill it. If we kill the cubs and they are not as big as the government says they must be, we will be in trouble with the Game Management Officer. . . ." Finally the men decided to shoot the free animal and take the skin to be measured, hoping to secure permission to kill the remaining cub. The hunters skinned the animals and cached the meat and the large skin. When they released the second cub and ran towards shore, he made straight for the spot where the remains of his mother and the other cub were cached.

The hunters did obtain the blessing of the Game Management Officer to shoot the little bear, and when they returned to do so he was still alive — thin but querulous.

Now, in the bright spring sunshine with the lines between shore and sea disguised by layers of drifted snow on and around the rough ice, I couldn't recognize the spot at all. Truly, my only aptitude for finding my way in the land of the Inuit is to do, unquestioningly, exactly what I'm told!

May

3 May

Just as I feared, I missed my trip by dog team.

After a week in Repulse Bay I had visited everybody twice, spent a day cleaning the principal's house — just like old times — and still there was no sign of Atani. After many cups of tea and circuitous conversations in many houses, I gave Simagak money to buy gas to take his wife to visit her sister — my friend Sila — in Igloolik — with me as an extra passenger. Early on the appointed day I took my duffel bag to his house as token that I was really serious about making the trip. A few hours later, as I placed another bag by Simagak's half-loaded qamutik, a plane flew over and came in to land.

At the strip I watched as the men helped the travellers pump fuel from forty-five gallon drums into the thirsty DC-3, and my ears pricked up as the name "Hall Beach" emerged from the buzz of conversation. I found the captain and, launching into a graphic description of the abuses to the human anatomy that days of land travel between Repulse Bay and Hall Beach would inflict, begged to be saved from the fate of such a trip. He listened sympathetically and didn't even flinch at my yelp of joy when he announced that he would not land at Hall Beach but go straight on to Igloolik. To his inquiry about accommodations at Igloolik, I explained about the Transient Centre where meals are provided, but where there would be no breakfast unless they took me along with them. "Well then, I guess you'll just have to come with us," he grinned.

I dropped my tote bag at the plane and rushed to extricate my bags from the load Simagak was just lashing down. He looked a bit confused but promised to bring me a carving worth the price of the fuel I had furnished for his trip. I staggered off, bearing my bags back to the airstrip where beaming crew members were returning from the Co-op, their wallets lightened and arms laden with the lovely miniature carvings for which the people of Repulse Bay are famous in art circles. As we lifted off the strip, there on the ice below us, just coming round the point, were Atani and his dogs. It had taken them fourteen days to complete the run from Igloolik. An hour and thirty-five minutes later we touched down on the Igloolik airstrip.

This is the first time I've noticed the horizon in a long time. I can now see through the newly frost-free window beyond the island to the hills of Melville Peninsula, rising blue-black beyond the brown-spotted snow of Igloolik. Temperatures drop below freezing every night and are unseasonably warm in the daytime, hovering around zero and causing snow to melt and evaporate. The old people say this is next month's weather. The frost lines have disappeared from the fuel tanks, Our Lady who stands above the entrance to the stone church has dropped her handful of snow (I wonder on whom), there is spring green in my water tank though I cleaned it recently. The cant of my house has changed, revealing a bit of spring sky between the window sash and the wall, and the door has become quite snug, requiring a harder pull or push than some of the smaller children can manage. At 3:00 A.M. I awoke and saw that the sky was pink on the horizon. I wondered if it were sunrise or sunset, but just closed my eyes and went back to sleep without solving the mystery.

4 May

Mystery solved. The dawn arrived at 4:00 A.M. with a young drunk. I had just put water on for coffee when Cindy — clad only in a pink shortie nightgown and black rubber boots — burst in from next door, pursued by a second drunk. We gave the men coffee then watched them stagger off before Cindy went home to bar her door pending the return of her husband from checking his nets. When I went to work this morning, I found one of the men curled up asleep in my porch.

Marcusi came to fill my water tank and stayed to feast on tea and walrus igunaq. He grimaced at the limburger cheese I offered him, saying "It smells rotten!" He talked about Inuit gastronomic delicacies, noting that the qallunaat appreciation of the polar bear hide has resulted in less of the tasty meat from bears killed in the fall when they are fat from summer feeding. Some hunters now prefer to kill spring bears whose pelts will bring good prices but whose meat has suffered from the animal's winter diet.

"We used to just kill a bear when we saw one" he chuckled wryly. "Now the government counts our bears and give us metal tags. The hunter now goes out looking for a bear, and we don't even wear much bearskin clothing any more!"

6 May

The Bay has an interesting selection of tanned furs for sale. In addition to wolf, coyote, and black bear strips for parka trim, there are raccoon tails and squirrel, rabbit, and cat hides. I asked Siaku what some of the pelts I could not identify might be. *"Amai,"* he shrugged, "but look!" he showed me a bolt of black, glossy-finished stuff with a quilted, white synthetic backing. He fingered the warm lining material appreciatively and declared, "It's excellent for snowmachine seat-covers."

An Inuk again reminded me of the Japanese I knew when a youngster from Repulse Bay sighed, "I want to go home because I miss Jusipi" — his three-year-old brother. It was not uncommon in Japan to see a teen-ager gently guiding a tiny tot through a park or department store with the same tenderness and devotion prevalent here between siblings.

7 May

This month the Radio Society has increased the scheduled broadcast hours. Ever since CBII-fm, Igloolik Comunity Radio, went on the air in January, 1976, the emphasis has been on "community." Not only do Inuit of all ages talk over the air — from the four-year-old wishing his brother a happy birthday to the elders telling tales of the old days — but an amazing percentage of the population also mans the controls. When they lived in camps, before their language was written, Inuit not only told the stories that are their history, but they wove the happenings of the day into scarey, thrilling, or humorous vignettes. Now they either broadcast the stories live or put them on cassettes.

The noon-time announcements sometimes run over the allotted fifteen minutes, and now, instead of coming on at 10:00 P.M., CBII broadcasts from 8:30 until midnight with a break for the territorial news. Those people who are concerned about the children's propensity to play all night then come home to sleep instead of going to school, feel it is a community, rather than a personal problem. Inuit did not tell their children to go to sleep when they lived in camps and they refuse to do so in the settlements. There are tales of days past when RCMP patrolled the streets sending youngsters home, when teachers went from door to door in the morning collecting students, and when the principal in Igloolik climbed on the school roof to ring a bedtime bell. Every spring when the days get long, some committee — School Advisory Board, Hamlet Council, or, this year, the Radio Society — decides there should be some effort to get the children to bed at night and to school during the day. Last month the radio came on the air at 10:00 P.M., and their first announcement was to ask people to send visiting children home to bed.

I was uneasy one day when Ikpunu was overly friendly in the store and sure enough, he came to visit that evening. I gave him four boxes of slides, took up my knitting and said very little. Children came in, played a while, and went out and more children came and still he stayed. He kept looking at his watch and I kept wishing he would leave. Finally at ten o'clock, when CBII broadcast its admonition for children to go home, he turned to them and told them to leave. I got up, smiled sweetly, and said, "You too. I go to work very early in the morning."

This noon there were the usual announcements: Coffee Shop hours; title of tonight's movie (another Kung-fu epic!); meetings of Alcohol Education Committee, Housing Association Board of Directors, Hunters' and Trappers' Association; someone asking for ujjuk for boots, and one of her children announcing that an old woman is home from the nursing station and would like some fresh fish. One man invited people to his house for boiled seal and another countered with an offer of cooked caribou.

10 May

Today I visited with Itu and Ningiu in their workroom. What a fairyland! Itu is working on yet another kayak, about eighteen inches long, of soapstone with all the accoutrements — hunter, harpoon, avataq, paddle — of soapstone or ivory with sinew for the lines. Ningiu was working on a summer scene. On the shoulder blade of a caribou she has glued bits of moss and pebbles around a fish-skin tent, secured by sinew ropes. Inside the tent is a sleeping area covered with lemming skin, a tiny bone ulu and a snow knife, a stone qulliq, and fur-clad figures sleeping or sitting. She has used fish vertebrae to edge the sleeping platform and fish ribs for tent supports. Itu has an old hassock and Ningiu a cushion on the floor. There is an array of homemade shelves all around the room with boxes, cans, and bags everywhere amid a jumble of tools dusted with pulverized stone, ivory, antler, and sawdust. From the shelves and out of the boxes pour every imaginable material: bird, lemming, and fish skins; bits of fabric; bones; animal skins and hair; pebbles, moss, feathers, lichens; dog, fox, walrus, whale, and caribou teeth; stone and ivory; antlers and tusks, whole and in pieces; marbles, beads, sequins, plastic tiddly-winks, broken knitting needles, pieces of wood — everything! The tools themselves are fashioned with antler handles by the carvers. Today, Ningiu picked up an ajagaq, which she handed to me after catching the vertebra on the rib handle four or five time in a row. Every time I caught it they oohed encouragingly, saying nothing the many times I missed. When I left, they told me laughingly, "Take it home and learn to do it like an Inuk."

When I got home, it took me some time to realize that what I thought was a peccadillo by the water delivery crew was really a leak in my fifty-gallon plastic water tank. I filled every large pan I have, the bath tub, and bucket, then Cindy and I carried buckets of water to her house. When Pita came from Housing to take the tank and patch it, he also took the dilapidated wooden box-type stand on which it sits. He was back a few hours later, bringing me a water tank with a spigot and my rebuilt box. Already I've caught myself lifting up the wooden circle that serves as a lid when I needed water, instead of using the faucet. As if to impress me with its presence, the spigot bit me on the leg when I walked too close to it.

13 May

For months there has been a sign on the washing machine in the Transient Centre, "This machine is out of order. If you wish to repair it, feel free to do so." A bored electrician waiting for his plane fiddled around with it and this morning showed me how to make it work.

When the machine is supposed to empty after the wash and rinse cycles, you change two wires from one connection to another.

One day when Inaq was at my house for coffee, I had talked to him about what kind of porch I would like to both affront the wind and weather and satisfy my aesthetic desires. The porch roof would have to be below the level of the house roof in order to avoid enclosing two high, small windows. Tonight I went to the Housing Association Board of Directors' meeting to ask for the porch. Inaq sketched what I wanted and as the drawing circulated, I offered to help with the construction. After a bit of discussion punctuated by laughter, the interpreter, eyes twinkling, said, "Yes, they will build the porch, but Inaq asks that you not try to help." Everyone burst out laughing.

On the way home I thought, the moon looks as if it were done with the wrong kind of paint. The landscape is done in pastels: blues on whites for the shadows on the snow; pink, mauve, and blue for the sky; darker pastels for the houses. Then the artist slapped on a moon in bright yellow acrylic.

17 May

Yesterday evening I caught Pita loading his gear to go seal hunting. After some verbal skirmishing he passed the buck to his partner, Toby, who answered *amai* to my request to go along. *Ii* is "yes." *Akka* is "no," and *amai* translates as, "I don't care to say," "I don't know." In this instance I decided it meant, "If you're around when we go I guess we'll have to take you along," and hurried off.

I burst into my house and hastily turned it upside down, strewing clothes, food, and gear all over. I donned several layers of clothing, starting with the long johns I had just finished knitting, and stuffed extra kamiks, duffel stockings, mitts and scarf, and a pound of raisins, a package of dried fruit, the remains of a box of crackers, camera, film, and metal cup into a small mail bag. By then Pita was gone, so I stumbled as fast as I could over to Toby's house. He was busy tying together an old, rather small qamutik with a couple of broken slats. I sat down next to Angut who was watching Toby finish packing.

When Toby went into the house I followed, explaining to the women that Pita had left me behind. They laughed. "Are you going with Toby?" My confusion caused more laughter while my would-be host stood finishing his tea. For the first time since his non-commital *Amai*, he spoke to me. *"Irngusiqaqpiit?"*

46

The question was so unexpected that I repeated the word to myself a couple of times *"Irngusiq? Irngusiq?"* but before I could find the translation — "Do you have a cup?" — Toby strode out with me padding along right behind him.

He started his machine, his eleven-year-old son Abraham and I flopped onto the sled, and away we went. And how! The single caribou skin and qulitaq strapped to the qamutik were not enough to soften the blows — and blows they were — as we went banging along behind the racing Yamaha. The driver was going as fast as he could; the qamutik was slamming down so hard over what, from shore, looked like smooth sea ice, that we ricochetted off the slats. . . . then — incredibly! — it got worse. I wondered how people survived such beatings unharmed, then I'd laugh and tell myself "I don't care. I'm glad I'm here." I'd start to form the words, then mentally grinning, would quickly clench my teeth for fear they'd sever my tongue. I concentrated on remaining relaxed, as if I were riding a horse, but this thing had a gait like no horse I've ever ridden.

When we caught up with Pita at the floe edge, his younger brother Johnny was with him, and on his qamutik was a plywood, home-made, flat-bottomed boat and a double-bladed paddle. I then realized Abraham could easily have gone on the skidoo with his father, who probably had fixed up the old sled just for me.

No one got the first seal we sighted. Pita said there would be no seals that day because of the wind. Toby stationed himself by the open water and had Abraham drive the machine around to flush seals out from under the ice. When that tactic didn't work, we played leap frog: first Toby's motor toboggan would follow Pita's, then Pita's would pull ahead, and so they progressed all the way along the lead. Riverside Drive. Sometimes there were mounds of ice beside the water, some-times just a clean break, and farther on, angular chunks tinted pale emerald green. Sometimes the water's edge curved, but at other places the ice had broken off at abrupt angles.

We stopped for short intervals several times without sighting seals, though there were huge flocks of ducks with a few seagulls mixed in. Pita and Johnny were stopped, rifles cocked. As we slowed down passing them, they yelled, "There! On the land. . ." Toby ran towards the water's edge, fired, and blew the middle out of a duck. Abraham tossed the remains on the qamutik and we continued along the water course, soon coming upon two more Inuit. As we chatted, another hunter grinned, tossed a salutation our way, and walked by to take up a position farther along. We were following Pita when our qamutik veered around so smoothly that when we stopped, close to the water, I was surprised to find we were facing the direction from which we had come. Our driver had been glancing at the water as he drove and had spotted a seal. He got it and the three of us waved to Pita to come back with the boat. Toby knelt in it, smoothly paddling kayak-style, with swift, sure strokes, retrieving the seal before it sank.

Ever since we had first caught up with them, Pita's refrain had been, "Let's have tea." Now the signal was given at last, but just as Johnny had the stove filled and primed and was about to light a match, the other men decided to push on. I think it was the black cloud forming over the floe edge that made them keep going. We went on beyond Qikiqtaarjuk, the peninsula on the other side of Igloolik Point, and there stopped for tea and fresh seal. The stomach flu bug which had stolen my appetite a couple of days before suddenly relented and let me enjoy liver and fat. While we were feasting, Pita spotted an animal far out and shot it. He came back standing, paddling stern first against the rising wind, and we were amused to hear him complaining and chattering as soon as he got within earshot. Toby grabbed the stern and jerked it onto the ice, throwing Pita off balance as both men laughed. Behind the craft he had dragged in a large seal.

Pita kept worrying for fear I was cold, but I was comfortable, except — of course — for my feet. They might as well belong to somebody else, for all the blood they get! But they weren't cold enough to spoil the trip for me.

As we came back across the island, there was a red slash on the horizon and I enjoyed looking at the blue mountains of Melville Peninsula. Unfortunately my eyeballs were bouncing against their sockets and now and then I would feel a dull headache. "Nothing serious," I told myself. "It's merely where my bones have slapped together." As the sled came to rest by the forty-five gallon drum that had been sitting on it before we left, I fumbled for my mail bag, tossed a "thank you" towards my host, and tottered off. I was home at thirty minutes after midnight. Toby popped in at eight this morning but didn't stay for coffee. On his way to work, he was just checking to be sure I'd survived. In the store this afternoon Pita inquired about my health. I did a little dance and wag to indicate how fit I am. The soreness in my spine will go away someday, and I guess I didn't really chip or bend anything beyond repair or refraction.

Sila came by with Larry, I suspect to see for herself what shape I'm in after the night's adventure, though ostensibly to tell me that the inspector is due next month to appraise the new houses. "The people will be going out on the land," I commented, thinking that her family would probably not move until the fall, when the Inuit bring their children back in for school. "When we move you will not visit so often," she half stated, half asked. "*Ii*" I agreed, "but you may stop in my house to get warm when you have such a long way to go to the stores." It was her turn to agree.

Mimi must have thought the washing machine was fixed to work normally, for the men at the Transient Centre tell me the hall was flooded last night. And to add insult to injury, they ran out of water. Fortunately, someone thought to turn off the pump so the hot water heater unit will not be burned out again. The original government houses like mine have fifty-gallon, plastic water tanks, some with and some without spigots. More recent models like the Transient Centre have two-hundred-and-fifty-gallon tanks providing water to a pressure system pumping hot and cold water to sinks. When water in my house falls below the spigot level I tip the tank to pour water into a bucket. When the water level in the Transient Centre tank falls below the pumping system pipes, I risk life, limb, and dignity hanging over the rim of the tank to scoop up enough water for morning coffee.

When the water truck was broken down for such a long time last February, the principal's wife hitched up her husband's qamutik to their Arctic Cat, grabbed her axe, and took me out to get ice at Ikpiarjuk Bay. The blocks along that shore are old ice that has drifted for years in Foxe Basin, then been driven into Turton Bay by a south wind, and trapped when the new ice formed last fall. By the time I had threaded my way around the cracks and through the soft snow, my benefactor was at work on top of a tower of ice. Fortunately, I received the first hunk on my foot instead of my head, and thereafter I stood well back, waiting for subsequent projectiles, which I carried to the sled while my partner loosened the next piece with a few well-directed blows of her axe. This tumble of blue ice dumped by my front door had gradually been buried in the snow, for — unlike the Inuit, who would have used it for tea until it was all gone — I have hoarded it, using it only when I ran out of water. Just last week I dug out the last bit to melt to wash my hair. The bulldozer just left the garage, going to fix the water lake road, so I'll take that bath I've been postponing.

18 May

It took me a while to identify the straight, narrow slashes, about a foot to a foot and a half long, in the snow. The clue was their position to leeward of the power poles. In this country power lines not only cast shadows, they sometimes leave tracks in the snow, and today they are spitting. It is warm again, almost raining. Every now and again the south wind rips the wet snow off a wire and flings it onto the snow-covered ground, as if playing jackstraws.

I never cease admiring nature's force and beauty, gentleness and power. The northwest wind usually prevails, moulding hard, perfectly even ridges, rounded like dunes of sea sand. Blowing snow, even if blue sky sometimes shows through, forms hard drifts with a few inches of pure white swirling dry stuff on top, not yet settled into the serious business of being a "real" snowbank. But for a week now we have had flurry after flurry of fluff borne on southeasterly winds. Instead of rippling the snow, the south wind tatts lacey lines which crumble at the slightest disturbance. It is messy, tiring, and treacherous to walk in.

Tonight, below my calves, where the meat thins out towards the bones, my legs are red from being beaten against the qamutik on the trip to the floe edge.

27 May

Temperatures are ranging between −15°C and 5°C and the disappearing snow reminds me of the tide going out. As it recedes, a host of things emerge: mittens, bones, boots, rocks, houses, boats. A patch of blue or green will spread and stretch, eventually becoming the keel of an overturned canoe. The revelations are still interesting rather than the eyesores they will be later on when the countryside stands completely brown instead of snow-speckled, as it is today. "Tidal pools" form on the main thoroughfare in the afternoon sun. During the night, when the sun is low and the air cools, the ponds freeze over, which accounts for the bike held fast in a deep cake of ice in front of the hamlet office. The crusts are still too thick for the children to break with their boots, but the morning traffic quickly grinds up the ice, which is then ready for the afternoon sun's work.

After school there was a group of children playing on the sea ice. One bike, in lieu of a front wheel, sported a toy-sized qamutik. It seemed hard to steer but no harder than the team of about eight dogs that five youngsters were trying to master. The dogs would finally start forward, the children would jump on the qamutik, and, in a moment, half the dogs would veer left, the other half right. Finally, they'd mill around and lie down in a bunch, and the driver would run at them, trying to make them move. One mutt would rise, tail wagging, and laconically wander towards his master.

The neatly stacked chairs, lying in long rows on their sides on the roof of the Community Hall, are another of the childrens' favourite toys. Players help themselves and soon form a procession, pushing chrome frames around town and down onto the ice. Other children appropriate the splintered pieces of wooden seats and backs to use for sledding on the hills.

At first glance, it seems that women from outside lavish time and interest on food, whereas the Inuit women are more concerned with clothing. With reliable phone service via satellite, gourmet cooking has become a hobby among temporary northerners in the eastern Arctic settlements served by jet plane from southern markets. The desirability of some foods is enhanced by their scarcity, thus one culture esteems the elusive truffle while another delects in the contents of the walrus stomach. Other foods earn their gourmet status from the manner in which they are prepared: eggs Benedict in some countries; igunar fish and meats in the land of the Inuit. It seems to take more time in the home to prepare most Euro-Canadian dishes than cooked Inuit foods. An exception to confirm the rule glows in my memory. After gathering mail bags full of mosses, willow, and lichens at Situqaqvik, Vira and I spent one summer afternoon, in the company of four or five children, tending an outdoor fire, carefully skimming the fat off the boiling pot every few minutes, to prepare char for Nulia in "the old way."

Different money management patterns and the Inuit trait of sharing with relatives and friends contribute to very different grocery shopping habits between the Euro-Canadian Igloolik housekeepers and their Inuit counterparts. The former will usually shop on the days the fresh produce arrives. Since a trip to the store is a time for Inuit to socialize, they keep little store-bought food on hand, replenishing their supply every day or two. One enterprising Inuk even did a brisk evening business selling canned milk and cigarettes at after hours mark-ups until his store burned down.

Much of the preparation of Inuit food is done by the hunter; a great deal more of the Inuit woman's time goes into making clothing — kamiks, duffel stockings, parkas and parka covers, caps and mitts, as well as hunters' skin clothing and boots. A native woman's family is the showcase for her embroidery, crocheting, knitting, and tailoring and Easter and Christmas provide the settings for undeclared, but nonetheless intense, competitions.

June

1 June

Suzie had a tooth filled today. She and Sally were envious of their elders who lived "in the good old days" when Inuit had strong, beautiful teeth with no cavities. The rotten teeth of today's young Inuit graphically show the results of dealing with a phenomenon from one culture with the methods of another. Sweets can cause unbrushed teeth to decay. But since children should be happy, they are allowed all the sweets they desire, brushing their teeth only if they wish. So there are four-year-olds whose teeth are no more than rotted, black stumps. The easy way out is to blame the unhealthy foods. Some of my two- and three-year-old friends who have been introduced to toothpaste like its taste and sometimes suck the brush instead of candy, which may later become a regular brushing habit. Suzie thought that having to brush her teeth at school turned her against brushing whereas Sally declared just the opposite and wished that her younger sister's teacher had brushes for each child, as her teacher had had when she was in the lower grades. Suzie remarked that her mother had beautiful teeth, adding, "I can remember her pulling sinew back and forth between her teeth when everyone else was smoking after eating." How I wish the Inuit I see using needles as toothpicks would use caribou sinew instead!

We all agreed that it is nice the old people can get dentures now and laughed at how most of them fumble among the clutter of their prized possessions to find them when they want to devour anything the least bit hard. I once saw a grandma postpone an anticipated morsel because the baby would not relinquish its new toy. When I left, the happily sucking baby was holding her bottle in one hand and waving the teeth in the other, wide-eyed, showing no signs of succumbing to the slumber that would free the prize and allow her patient granny to dine.

Each of us had a story. Mine was of the Repulse Bay woman who used to keep her denture under her pillow until it went through the wringer in a pillow slip, altering both the rollers on the washing machine and the fit of the teeth.

"When Pangok lost another tooth," Sally related, "he carved himself a replacement of ivory and carefully fitted it in with the others on his bridge."

"Remember when Attia's husband went to Pond Inlet and took the box containing all their teeth?" laughed Suzie. "She told everyone over the radio, that she would only eat babies' food until he got back."

We decided Siuti gets the most out of her false teeth. During the several years I have known her, her lower plate has been broken in the middle. If she wishes to deal with anything more than soft food, she expertly installs a section of teeth and gingerly chews in that area, using the piece of partial plate like a tool — which indeed it is! — as someone else would use finger, knife, or fork. In anticipation of a particularly succulent treat, she will glue her lower plate together the previous day, then laugh and chat while feasting, until the fateful moment when *crr ~ aa ~ ck* announces she must once again confine her gourmet experiences to one side of her mouth. Typically, when the instrument is in working order, she makes no effort to restrain her ebullience, enjoying her repast to the utmost, even though this possibly precipitates an early end to that delectation. A less flamboyant eating style would prolong the life of the repair job, but it would mean less intense delight. In the old days the rationale would have been; gourmandize while you may for tomorrow there may be nothing: today it is; eat lustily, for at any moment you may be pulled up short by a *snap-crack.*

After Sally's remark that her father's teeth are white after he brushes them, I'm sure I'll never again be able to see Inaq's grin without checking to see what colour it is.

5 June

Toby and Tommy are packing the huge qamutik and Natika the smaller one for their trip to Arctic Bay. There is a mound of clothing in the middle of the living-room floor, through which Sila is pawing, selecting duffel socks, kamiks, boots, and other clothing for each of the children. Tutu is sewing, repairing the items her mum gives her, and Rebecca, with Larry in the amauti, is doing laundry. Sita runs and dives into the pile of clothing like a southern boy his age would burrow into a pile of fall leaves, and Sila tries to shoo him away. Ivo escapes with his guitar, and I can see Abraham running towards the beach with his peers, throwing bolos at the seagulls. Even I am infected by the excitement and wish I could go along.

7 June

On my way to the Co-op I walked behind an amauti-clad Inuk with a baby on her back. The woman wore spring boots of white canvas with ujjuk soles, embroidered duffel stockings, and — sparkling in the sun below her amauti — a knee-length, gold lamé dress.

Later I went for a walk with an empty bucket and came back from the far side of the island with gold of my own in the shape of enough moss, flowers, and willow plants to crowd my little house, and dirt in which to grow lettuce and chard.

When I got home, much to my delight the men from the Housing Association were installing a 150-gallon fuel tank instead of the 45-gallon drum that has fed the little stove used for cooking and heating my house. Even if the new fuel truck does not arrive on sealift this fall as expected, I look upon that dear tank as my insurance against another chilling performance like that of last January. My house froze up three times in one week, and once more for good measure the following week. Everything had conspired to allow me the honour of setting some kind of record that I do not wish to duplicate.

First of all, we in snug Foxe Basin, usually protected from the howling winds that circulate around Hudson's Bay, were treated to storms of a frequency and intensity that made the old people scratch their memories to recall a similar plague. The pump on the Co-op fuel truck broke first, and while that was being fixed, oil was hand-pumped from forty-five-gallon barrels on sleds. More fuel was required because of the unusual cold and wind, causing tanks to run dry before their turn came to be refilled. When the pump was fixed, the delivery truck was sometimes immobilized, waiting for the snowplough to clear a way through the latest set of snowbanks. Soon the delivery men were unable to supply fuel before the tanks emptied, for they were busy day and night running from one cold house to another. Then the truck, already a bit wobbly, collapsed under the additional strain, leaving the contractor to resort once again to forty-five-gallon drums on qamutiks.

The first time my stove quit it was fourteen hours before I again had heat. There was no real damage: the thin layer of ice on the water tank was no problem, a jar of pickles froze and broke, and the cork in a bottle of wine rose without the help of a corkscrew. That night I discovered my electric blanket was broken, but by morning I was too warm in my down sleeping bag.

Two days after the men had delivered fuel, the stove again quit. The Co-op assured me I could not be out of oil so soon despite the freezing cold, and suggested I call Housing Association. A few hours later a man came to work on the stove, and in only six hours the house was once more cosy. Three days later I turned the stove up as I went off to cook breakfast, for the wind had risen during the night and the house was a bit chilly. When I returned, entering in a whirl of snowy wind, the house was more than chilly; it was again icy.

I went over to Sila and Toby's house to use their phone. "Call Saati," was their advice. Toby phoned the delivery man's house for me, spoke briefly, hung up, and told me, "Saati is sleeping." I drank tea and played with the baby, keeping an eye on my house and fidgeting as drifts began to form. When Toby came home for coffee-break, I asked him when he thought Saati might come. *"Amai,"* was his answer, "his wife said he was sleeping." Then it dawned on me that she would not waken him as I had assumed she would; that I must wait, probably with others who ran out of fuel during the day, while Saati slept. I told myself sternly that the fuel men were having a worse time than I, tried to be nonchalant like the Inuit in the same situation, and went off to visit friends in warm houses.

The wind dropped, the snowplough made its rounds; Saati awoke and filled my tank around six in the evening. My stove was lit and I went off to seven o'clock mass thinking to come home to a warm house. Not so! The stove had gone out! When I tried to relight it I discovered a pool of oil in the fire pit. So I donned my dirty camping sweatshirt and sopped up the fuel with newspapers. Still the fire would not take, so — as usual — I called on Toby for help. He adjusted this bolt and that, turned a screw here and another there, fiddled around with the carburetor, and finally coaxed a flame into the fire pit. It was almost midnight when he packed up his tools and went home.

At 2:00 A.M., when my cold nose alerted me to a dead fire, I pulled on my wind-pants and parka over my pyjamas, put on my kamiks, grabbed my sleeping bag, and stumbled over to Toby's house. Abraham was asleep on the living-room couch so I settled down on the floor near the space heater. Toby was the first one astir in the morning, nodding a greeting as he went into the bathroom. I turned my face to the wall, concentrated on ignoring the morning sounds, and dozed off for a while as the children prepared for school. However, I could not ignore the blast of cold air when Toby's brother-in-law came in. He sat down at the table, poured himself some coffee, cast his eyes towards me, and queried, "What's she doing here?"

The following week, when the stove went out yet again, one of the teachers suggested that the fuel might be too cold to burn. He rigged up an electric light bulb over the valve where the fuel line came into the house and I insulated the outside pipe from the barrel to the house with some salvaged fiberglass insulation. It worked! The stove stayed on — my midnight rambles to the neighbours seemed to be over. Now that I have a real tank instead of a barrel, I will ask Housing to replace the short, straight fuel feed-pipe with a coiled line whose extra length will give the fuel time to warm up before it hits the fire.

Anna is back washing dishes and cleaning at the Transient Centre, with her fourteen-year-old daughter Martha sometimes helping her, and two-year-old Rosa toddling around the place. Last year they lived in Hall Beach where her husband has relatives. She tells me they came in last week by Skidoo and are living in a one-room "match box" until something larger is vacated during the big shuffle, when people move into the new houses. Her husband Tugala is small but strong and always looks quite jaunty, with a shock of wavy hair falling across his forehead and the pompom of his bright crocheted cap bobbing saucily to one side. I don't know whether he is shy or just prefers not to speak Inuktitut with me since I understand so poorly. We exchange silent smiles when our paths cross, but Anna always stops to chat. Though she seems disappointed that my Inuktitut has not improved more, I still find her easy to be with. She is so eager to learn, watching what I do with the food as she cleans the kitchen. When I showed surprise that she had a daughter as old as Martha, she laughed and named the rest of her children — four girls and three boys with two years between each.

The children are already excited by the prospect of spring camp — the last two weeks of school when the entire student body, with teachers and parents, moves out on the land. The official dates, set with an eye to the plane schedule, are from Friday the fourteenth until Friday the twenty-eighth, allowing the teachers to catch the Friday night plane south. Recess gatherings in the school staff room find the new teachers being admonished by old hands, "Don't forget flints and lighter fluid," "Be sure to bring tools and spare parts . . . ," or making mental notes as anecdotes unfold; the list of people succoured one after the other by one teacher's extra pair of wind-pants, the principal's humorously woeful account of the liquidation of his two-week supply of peanut butter in one tea-drinking, story-telling orgy only hours after their arrival. . . .

Students are asking their favourite teachers to come with them, people are deciding in which of the old campsites they will set up their tents, and everyone is watching the weather, speculating about which will be the best place for seal or caribou hunting, fishing, or gathering eggs. But first there will be the annual school picnic at Avvajja, scheduled for next Wednesday, weather permitting.

14 June

The school picnic was a great success as usual. Children were allowed only five hot dogs apiece, but after the bannock was gone, the supply of pilot biscuits and sweet tea was unlimited. This year there was a mud-patch, surrounded by snow, on which people played the Inuit version of baseball, and there were blue puddles on the sea ice between the island and the mainland point of Avvajja, the traditional site of the outing. Though the snowbanks were shrinking, children managed to climb onto the roof of the remains of the original Roman Catholic Mission. Even little scamps walked carefully around the mounds of rocks in the cemetery, while I wrote down those notations I could still read from the wooden crosses.

15 June

The island is criss-crossed with snowmobile tracks leading to the various trails heading out to Nirlirnaqtuq and other nearby islands, Baffin Island, or Melville Peninsula. During the nights, when the sun dips low on the horizon and temperatures drop to ten or fifteen degrees below freezing, qamutiks mounded with tents, food, fuel, hunting equipment, personal belongings, and people will lurch over the pack ice behind straining machines, then glide quickly out of sight across the relatively smooth sea ice. After their winter confinement in the settlement, the people eagerly seize any excuse to be on the land. Seal hunting parties head for the floe edge, families set out to visit in Repulse Bay or Pond Inlet and picnicking couples, like shuttles, weave their tracks among the trails of the serious travellers.

On the noon radio show today were calls for rubber boots (size 11), snowmobile parts, ujjuk for kamiks, and a plea to borrow a camp-stove, interspersed with invitations to eat boiled meat at Itu's, fish at another home, or frozen, raw caribou at a third. Lately, happy customers have lugged home treasures from the rummage sales of teachers, RCMP, and the lab manager, who are returning south, or the Inuit who are moving north to the mining town of Nanisivik.

The gently sloping roofs of houses, still easily accessible by snow-bank, are a favourite place for bike riding now that the few dry spots on the muddy roads have been pre-empted by hopscotch players. While the adults are busy preparing for camp, little children make traps for snow buntings and gulls, and bigger boys seem more successful at bringing down their quarry with sealskin slingshots than with their jerry-built bows and arrows and spears. The movement in the settlement is unsettling me, and I'm tempted to see if someone won't take me out to camp.

25 June

My turn to go camping came at last. A week ago yesterday Jeannie took me out to Siuraarjuk, then came to bring me back last Sunday. My proposition had been to pay for the gas needed to transport me somewhere — anywhere there was a camp! — and bring me back in. The hunters I know best — Toby, Inaq, Pita, Tugala, Tukilaq — were all planning only one trip with their large families, so had no room for me and my gear. One of them would probably have taken me out when he came in to the settlement to sell furs and renew his supplies, but I particularly wanted to enjoy the ambience when the people first get out on the land after the long winter in the settlement.

I quit approaching hunters I don't know very well when one asked me to buy a forty-five-gallon barrel of fuel for the trip to nearby Nirlirnaqtug, when five gallons would have sufficed. He added, with a big grin, pointing to the seventeen-year-old slouched in the corner,

"You can sleep with my son!" I was venting my frustration to Jeannie when she announced, "Go buy the gas. I'll take you out Friday after work." I should have known she would love a chance to go off somewhere, but I had been thinking of men. An airline used to advertise "Getting there is half the fun," and so it was with Jeannie. Her husband packed our gear on their qamutik, helped us onto the sea ice and waved good-bye as we set off around 7:00 P.M.

As we left the settlement a wisp of white cloud rose from the horizon fanning out into a fluffy plume against the pale blue sky of the June night. Igloolik was barely out of sight when a black spot detached itself from the blue and white shadows of the rumpled sea ice. As the spot grew larger it separated into a snow machine — Tugala's — with a roundly loaded sled, and a cluster of figures. Several hunters had left their families enjoying tea on the trail while they made a quick side trip to the floe edge. Almost before Tugala cut his motor, the older children tumbled off the sled, running to join the group around the camp stove drinking tea. As we pulled up alongside, two smaller children slid off the caribou skins covering the load and made their way towards the others, while Anna shook the sleeping baby into a more comfortable position in her hood and tucked the caribou clothing securely around four-year-old Tina, nestled fast asleep against the tucker box. By the time Anna had joined the tea party, the surrounding ice was dotted with boys and girls playing tag. Twelve-year-old Mina had returned to the sled, and, rummaging through the food box, retrieved a two-burner camp stove, tea kettle, snow knife, canisters of tea and sugar, and several metal mugs varying in size, state of wear, and cleanliness. She pumped the stove, placed it carefully in the lee of the sled, and as she lit it Pita roared up on his Skidoo.

"Ujjuk at the floe edge," he announced gulping the tea someone had poured for him, and was gone. Tugala had no sooner gulped down a mug of sweet tea than he slipped his rifle strap over his shoulder, unhooked the qamutik from his machine, and raced after the black dot that was Pita speeding southwards to where the vapour billowed dark blue above the open sea.

Mina chose a wind-whipped tongue of snow, scraped off the surface and with quick chops of the snow knife packed the kettle full before running off to play. Anna tended the kettle, filling it several times as the snow shrank to water, then added several tea bags. As soon as the water boiled she set the kettle on the unlit burner and dug into the tucker box for more pilot biscuits.

The rising wind tumbled the emptied red-and-white biscuit box across the snowy plain. Tina stirred, sat up, surveyed the scene, then grumpily slid off the sled demanding tea. She whined and tugged at her mother's amauti. "I want tea," the child wailed, pummelling her mother with mittened fists and roaring her loudest at Anna's "Ssh . . . listen," as the buzz of a machine grew louder.

While the newcomers, Kinakiar and Tali chatted with Anna and Jeannie, their four youngsters inspected the work of Tugala's five older children who had stamped out pictures in the snow, then all the children gathered around the adults. Eight-year-old Mosha, squatting down in front of his pouting sister, Tina, received a kick and a cuff as thanks for his efforts to coax a smile from her. Tali contorted her face, swept the child off her feet, and, hugging her to her breast, bent her face into the child's parka hood muttering nonsense while rocking the little girl, who couldn't keep from laughing. As Tali set Tina down, she tendered a mug of well-sugared tea and broke a pilot biscuit in half so that the child could dip it into her drink.

Kinakiar was but another dot approaching the other seal hunters by the time Tali's cup was filled and she, Anna, and Jeannie perched on the qamutik chatting. One of her boys produced a box of pilot biscuits, a tin of butter, and a knife from their stores — provisions devoured by all the children in short order. When another game of tag was started, Mosha ran up and tapped Tali whose hand shot out to tag the tagger. Mosha stopped, backed off a few steps, then the contestants exchanged a swift round of tags until Mosha touched Anna and bolted out of reach. The woman was on her feet in a flash, joining in the game. Tali too was enticed into the fun but soon withdrew to the qamutik to change the squirming baby on her back. Jeannie took her place in the game as Tali dropped the wet disposable diaper on the snow at her feet, tucked the baby back into its nest, and bounced from one foot to another, patting the baby's bottom behind her back to calm its protests.

An hour or so later, at the approach of two snowmobiles, the women again lit the camp stove and filled the kettle. The men told of Urqsu's battle to keep a huge ujjuk and the hunter's small skiff afloat. "We didn't stay to eat," proclaimed Kinakiar, loosening the lashing ropes at the end of his qamutik. He plunked a five-gallon can of fuel down behind the machine and tossed a haunch of frozen caribou onto the snow. The children came running, some poking at the meat with their fingers while the others dug once more into the food boxes for knives. Older children expertly sliced off strips of the red feast for the younger ones and even Tina, with her mouth stuffed full of the crunchy frozen meat, was happy. Machines and people replete, the drivers sped off towards Siuraarjuk, now racing, now driving side by side, now nosing one snowmobile against the end of the other's qamutik while its passengers waved and grimaced amid shouts and bursts of laughter.

During the days at Siuraarjuk I spent lots of time hiking, climbing, and just sitting perched on a rock in the sun, absorbing the beauty around me and often taking notes on a tiny pad I stuck in a boot when I wasn't wearing pockets. As the snow retreated under the assault of the sun and the dry air, deep snowbanks on the sides of hills became treacherous pits of ice crystals which closed, vice-like, around foot and leg. Several times I dug myself out of such banks, but just two days before Jeannie came to take me home, on the hill just above my tent, I lost my notebook and pencil to one of the voracious snow pits. I'm sure my most luminous, intelligent, and poetic remarks were washed away in that melting snow, but here are some notes that survived. . . .

18 June

Tukilaq took Alita out seal hunting, though there is still much snow on the sea ice. They spotted a yearling basking beside its aglu. When the seal tried to dive to safety, snow had blocked the breathing hole and it lay frantically scratching at the ice and snow as the hunters approached. Tukilaq grabbed the seal by the tail, flipped it away from the aglu, and told five-year-old Alita to kill it. The young hunter timidly harpooned the animal, which snarled at him, making him retreat quickly, thus relinquishing the labour of the kill to Tukilaq. Upon their return, the whole camp admired the harpoon wound and made much of Alita, while his father skinned the animal. After his mother had boiled some meat, everyone brought their knives and ulus and feasted together in honour of Alita's first seal. Sara enjoyed a raw eye, eating the carefully peeled-off membranes first, then sucking out the juices through a neat slice at the bottom of the eyeball. She gave the inner clear spheroid to the little boy, and his grandmother showed him how to use it as a magnifying glass.

19 June

As I sat here facing the side of the tent and using a box as a writing table, a muzzle poked at the canvas. I ran my finger over it and heard the gravel rattle as it moved away. Then the shadow of a leg appeared and, as it was raised, I struck, sending the beast away with a yip.

Later, when I headed for the lake in the highlands, pail and cup in hand, I came upon six-year-old Patti (short for Patrick), and seven-year-old Sita and Alita. "Let's follow Georgia." Over the rocks, wobbling in my footprints in deep snow, across the tundra we went. Patti cried, "There's a raven's nest over there!" and we set off with him in the lead. On and on, but no nest, so I turned back for water. My young companions came too, discovering and dismantling avinngaq holes, turning over rocks and playing Don't-Step-in-the-Water and Don't-Touch-a-Rock. If they performed the forbidden act they had to tag me to get back in the game. At camp I learned that the field of deep snow we had crossed was the lake I had been vainly seeking.

Yesterday evening Atani, his wife, mother, sister, and three of his children came to visit with Urqsu, then left to set up camp at Uqsuutikkuvik to the east, while Urqsu returned to Igloolik. This evening, over the radio, Urqsu said hello to all of us at Siuraarjuk and Uqsuutikkuvik, and told us he had got two seals on his way home.

20 June

The sun commands a clear sky and a strong northwest wind continues for the second day. The mercury has climbed above zero and rivulets are running from deep snow drifts. The white snow cover on the sea ice opens into larger and larger lakes of blue as the sun and wind lose the battle to evaporate the torrents.

At 1:30 P.M. we set out to hunt seals. In front of Tugala on the motor toboggan is his son Patti, dressed in waterproof wind-pants, a down parka, and his mother's handiwork of cat-skin mittens and sealskin kamiks like his father's. On the qamutik are twelve-year-old Jackie, fourteen-year-old Martha, and me. We all wear down parkas, Martha saucy in the bright red qalipaaq made by her mum. She and Jackie wear heavy shoepacs while I'm glad to have found a pair of rubber boots big enough to accommodate my knee-length, caribou-skin stockings. Little Patti and I peer out from fur ruffs, the young people sport tuques when they are not bareheaded, and Tugala is dashing in a Montreal Expo's baseball cap, over which he rarely pulls his parka hood. The adults all wear leather mittens, mine hand-sewn of moosehide with duffel liners, the others store-bought.

Jackie helps push the sled through puddles and over rocks as we set out but soon jumps onto the tucker box at the rear. Martha flops down beside me on the lashed-down caribou skin and falls asleep, lulled by the purr of the motor toboggan and the shushing of soft, wet snow. Now and then we bounce over a protruding slab of ice or the song of the runners rises to a whine as we scrape over bare ice. Tugala stops the machine and calls for Jackie to come sit behind him. The boy's added weight gives us more traction, but it also pushes the caribou-skin slush-guard down onto the snow, where it follows limply instead of jauntily flopping as before. Several times we slow down, having spotted seals basking on the ice, but they are skittish in the spring and slither into their holes, out of reach, before we have even come close.

We stop, and Patti — carefully straining to put his feet in Tugala's footprints — follows his father up a mound of jagged ice blocks from which our guide scans the sea and land through binoculars. "There are four men walking on that hill," he announces, and I realize that we have passed Atani's camp at Uqsuutikkuvik. To my untrained eyes white tents pass for more patches of snow on the few small expanses of brown shore.

"Don't you want to make tea?" Tugala asks Jackie as he unhooks the snowmobile. Patti opts to go with his father to look for seals, Jackie and Martha deal with the camp stove, and, after filling the tea kettle with snow, I head for the last spot where we had seen a seal vanish. I walk for what seems like a long time and quite far — indeed, when I look back the teen-agers and the qamutik are very small and the snowmobile is but a black fleck on the blue-and-white expanse — but I find no trace of the breathing hole and wonder if I have even come near it.

When I rejoin the group, the pound of raisins I had jammed into my metal mug — my only hunting gear — are savoured by all, until Patti appropriates the bag, visibly enjoying those that remain.

The brisk wind and bright sunshine continue as we set out again and slowly approach several seals, all of whom dive back into the water before we are even within firing range. This time, when Tugala stops, he makes for the nearby shore. With his feet, he pats snow around cracks, making a safe path for Patti while the rest of us wade puddles and jump cracks in the ice. When we start to flounder in deep drifts, we fall in line walking behind Tugala up the long slope from the shore. On the top of the hill, just emerging from the snow, stand the remains of three qarmats. Tugala tells how the people who lived there had no camp stoves but used qulliqs, had no matches but struck sparks from rocks. In my halting Inuktitut I marvel at the cleverness of his ancestor who could survive with so little. When we get back to camp Tugala's wife Anna tells me, "My husband built one of those sod huts. His grandparents and my parents lived in the others." I am stunned, for I do not think of Tugala as very old, but I suppose the real surprise is that people much younger than myself, people among whom I live a village life, have lived "the old way," surviving through traditional skills.

We got no seals but returned smiling. We had had a nice day. Maybe tomorrow's hunt will provide meat. Tonight we will eat macaroni and cheese and tinned fruit cocktail.

21 June

It is most difficult in a large camp, in this treeless land, to find the privacy in which to relieve oneself. Tents, like iglus, are all equipped with toilet cans varying in size with the number of occupants, and several tents here boast white enamel chamber pots. However, the scene below is reward enough for those who disdain the pots and fight their way through compacting snow to the crest of the hills.

Gravel and sand are emerging from the sparkling snow of Siuraar-juk, which means "lots of sand." Rivulets sing as they dance their way to the shore, clearing the land around them; some make beautiful, gurgling music around the rocks under the snow. Clear, frozen collars encircle boulders as the snow pulls away from them under the high sun, then close in again as the mercury drops when the sun is low in the west.

Far out on the sea ice-blue puddles are spreading, while, on white hummocks close to shore, snowmachines and qamutiks lie in a jumble like pick-up sticks. Playing children jump the gullies made by melt-water streams from the land while teen-aged boys, alone or in pairs, rifles slung across their shoulders, trudge off across the tundra. On one side of a tiny brook, three tents balance on grey patches floating in the snow like frogs on lily pads. Across the stream, six more home-made white wall tents, some with rounded ends, tower over a green plastic children's play tent and a low-slung, two-tone, nylon creation — from the catalogue — with contrasting fly rippling and snapping in the wind. Back from the shore, where gravel succumbs to tundra, several seal skins are pegged out to dry. Everywhere barrels appear like punctuation marks: half-buried in the sand, emerging from snow banks and sea ice, stacked and topped with a pole holding aloft a radio antenna, in a neat row anchoring a tent, tipped on end for tables or play areas, and two support a qamutik balanced on its side, over which the women have hung strips of dark red caribou meat to dry into nikku and bright orange arctic char to dry into pissi.

Anna gets out her sewing machine and fashions a new front for their tent while Tugala saws and files, patiently shaping a harpoon head from scrap metal salvaged from the DC-3 aircraft that burned on the Igloolik airstrip several years ago. Tukilaq has tuned his motor toboggan and is making another seal hook while his wife Sara scrapes the skin of a seal — the sole fruit of the night's hunt. The old seals are as wary as the young ones are skittish. A yearling, alone on the ice by an glu, is the prize quarry, for the meat is tasty and the fur good for clothing or to sell. The skins of the older animals are scraped on both sides to be used as legs for waterproof boots.

The small children squeal with delight as a band of eight- and ten-year-olds return from a foray bearing a dead seagull — victim of their stones — and a very vociferous baby raven dripping lice. The wingspread of the gull is almost as wide as my outstretched arms. The boys prop up slabs of limestone, making a pen for the hapless raven, to whom they feed huge chunks of raw caribou. Letia hangs out laundry on the tent ropes as Pita emerges, yawning and stretching, strolls onto the sea ice, and surveys the scene as he relieves himself.

23 June

The sound of motor toboggans mingled with voices of greeting wafted into my sleep without completely rousing me so that when I looked out this Saturday morning, I was not surprised to find that several more tents had sprung up around me. Most are of white canvas though there is one of tan and blue parka cover material. Johnny's dogs occupy a strip of gravel surrounded by snow while the shreds of orange plastic that will shelter the teen-aged dog owner hunch nearby. Johnny's sister-in-law, Letia intermittently sews at the fabric until Sunday, when all work stops. By then it has assumed the shape of a small tent. Couples and families continued to arrive all day and night yesterday until there were fourteen tents clinging to the gravel patches between the quickly shrinking snowbanks. The weekend has been sunny and moderately windy with temperatures hovering near zero — perfect weather to evaporate snow and toss up mirages like shimmering white high-rises dancing in the distance.

The ice in front of the camp is spotted with qamutiks lying a rope's length behind their machines, more obedient than the dogs. A team lolls in their harnesses, occasionally rousing the pets to join their chorus or relieving their boredom with a quick fight, marked by the shrill screaming of the vanquished, cringing, belly-up, under the bared teeth of the snarling victor. Nine out of ten pet dogs are named Paapi, an Inuk child's rendering of "puppy." Pets used to be the puppies destined for dog teams, but with the arrival of the white man and his prolific pooches, mixed breeds abound. There are several tied around the camp. One resembles a border collie, another is a black, sleek mutt of German shepherd lineage with a feathered tail, and there's taffy-coloured Taffy, long of tail and leg with a Persian lamb hair-do.

The sole remaining family on the other side of the stream moved to our side, onto a choice waterfront lot recently relinquished by the snow. Now that the nights also are warm, the stream flows constantly, swelling quite respectably as the sun feeds it the drifts between the beach and the hills.

A night and day of strong winds shaking and grabbing at the tents succeeded in felling some aerials. Most tents have battery-operated radios, and several sport aerials poked through holes cut for that purpose and strung to poles brought from Igloolik and propped up by rocks on barrels. Fallen aerials are re-erected as soon as the wind dies. There are usually some people awake by noon when CBII-fm comes on the air broadcasting weather and ice conditions near the settlement, arrival and departure information for people travelling between camps and the settlement, any local news such as births and — above all — greetings.

Shortly after noon on Saturday, Tugala set out with his wife and four or five children. Tukilaq and his twelve-year-old son Jamisi manned a Moto-ski and qamutik, and Pita followed with his machine, towing Alita and me aboard his sled. We passed a woman, baby on her back, poised at an aglu, while her five-year-old proudly cruised with the Skidoo to flush seals for his mum. Tugala's bunch spread out at aglus but we went on. Many seals slipped into their holes as we approached and when Pita finally shot one, it sank before we

could get to the aglu to recover it. Eventually we found a den —
several breathing holes opening into a large ice cave. Pita and Alita
took up positions at the den, and Tukilaq, Jamisi, and I stationed
ourselves at more distant aglus, some of us wielding seal hooks since
there were not enough harpoons for everyone. When we got back
empty-handed at 4:30, the others had already returned, and some
women were flensing skins.

Kinakiar and family had arrived from their fish camp around 8:00
A.M., pitched their tent, and gone to sleep. While we were out on the
ice, some of the women in the camp had prepared many of Kinakiar's
fish to dry. The heads are cut off, then the fish are gutted and split
lengthwise along the backbone to the tail. The backbone is removed,
and the flesh is scored lengthwise and crosswise to the skin. The two
strips of skin, still joined at the tail, can then be easily hung over a
pole or tent rope or laid out to dry on rocks or boards.

Some campers have left and others have come. On the pebbles by a
sled, among the boxes and bags of gear, sits a gorgeous soapstone
carving, the forms blocked out but not yet finished: two Inuit and two
dogs attacking a polar bear which is staggering backwards. Powerful!
Alive! A twenty-four-year-old office worker started it and has given it
to his younger brother to finish.

24 June

A bunch of rowdies has moved in across the stream and are just
starting to function as I crawl into my sleeping bag. The teen-aged
boys roar around on snowmachines and the young parents can be
heard yelling at the children, "Don't touch the raven," "Don't pee
there," "Put that down." Even the baby screams. Around 8:00 A.M.
they quiet down. There are always people abroad in the summer
daylight: children playing, men coming in from or going out hunting,
women sewing, scraping skins, or just visiting over tea. Some people
sleep a few hours, go for a few, then sleep again. The boisterous ones
are the more noticeable for being an exception to the normal camp
behaviour of coming and going without disturbing those about you.

Just as the young people quieted down, Pita left for Igloolik to buy
groceries and gas and to sell some seal skins and the carving he has
made. His wife Letia and daughter Natar did a thorough tent-cleaning
in his absence, even hauling in mail-bag-loads of gravel. Next door,

Anna cut out pieces of caribou skin with her ulu, and, with sinew, sewed warm stockings for baby Rosa, who played on the sleeping skins at the back of the tent until her new footwear was ready. Outdoors, rubber boots made fine buckets as the other children — unmindful of the near-freezing temperature — busied themselves burying each other in sandy gravel.

Jeannie and Uinga arrived with their pet dog Baby, to the great delight of Pita's three six-week-old pups, who thought she was their mother returned. The pups spent hours playing fiercely under the qamutik where Baby was tethered, looking most comical as they stuck their heads up through the slats of the sled.

Alita strode purposefully off towards a small lake, towing a seal's hind flippers and tail, as Patti came down the hill triumphantly cradling a second baby raven. Now that the lake ice has disappeared several species of ducks, loons, terns, jaegers, and other sea birds have started building their nests.

If I were a musician I would write a Camp Symphony. The night movement would feature the rouffling of one edge of my tent fly in the wind (tenor saxophone), the melody shifting with the wind to the ra-ouffling of the other fly edge (alto saxophone), punctuated with dog howls (oboes), with puppy yip counterpoints (piccolo). The underlying theme would be the undulating wind (viola), rhythmic, persistent, waxing and waning. When the winds merely whispered, the gurgling of the tiny brook (flute) would be heard but soon submerged in the melody of the wind and its pranks with the tent fly.

The basis of the daytime movement would be the gentle, sparkling melody of sun on snow (violin). The brook theme would be heard, intermingled with the calls and laughter, mostly of children (bells and triangle), the whirr of snowmachines (drums and pizzicato strings), sometimes pulling qamutiks through slushy sea ice (brushes on cymbals and drums). Footsteps in the gravel, the clink of carvers working stone with chisel, the bonk of a caribou-skin ball hitting an oil drum, the muted hiss of camp stoves in tents, rising momentarily as the tent flap opens, then closes, the cries of birds echoed by the children's imitations; all are sounds to be included, gradually fading once more into the night wind theme.

So now I am home again, typing by the window which I slide open when Mimi stops to chat on her way to the store, remarking woefully,

"There are no people." The few of us left in the settlement seem to go out of our way to cross paths and exchange greetings. In the warm morning sun even the tiny yellow butterflies are safe, for the children have just gone to sleep after prowling throughout the night, fishing through the cracks in the bay ice or hunting lemmings in the tundra behind the village. Only one team remains tethered on the ice, the dogs enthroned on shrinking hummocks of dirty snow poking above water muddied by the winter's accumulation of turds and regurgitated fur balls.

I was feeling sorry for the dogs until the nice lady at the Transient Centre, doing some kind of research about Inuit, pointed out their plight to me. She reminded me of the middle-aged anthropology summer student at Rankin Inlet — so long ago that I was still trying to reason with such people — admonishing a four-year-old not to throw rocks at the birdies. I tried to point out that he was merely playing at being an adult in a society which still admires the hunter. The southerner acted as if only a demented sadist could have invented my tale that the child's parents probably encouraged his behaviour and praised him if his missive hit the target. Visitors who cannot temporarily disregard their own cultural formation and viewpoints in order to enjoy the differentness of the North sadden me. But people working or living in the North who refuse to adjust their perceptions to the new realities which might help them understand, if not accept, Inuit behaviour, madden me.

28 June

The carving that was at Siuraarjuk is in the Co-op now, beautifully finished and selling for $3,500.

July

1 July

The stores and offices are closed today for the holiday, but the atmosphere in the settlement is no different than it has been during the past two weeks. The few people in the village wander around with a general festive air all the time, for there is the daily excitement of people coming and going from the camps. More important than Canada Day was family allowance day last week. After the radio announcement of the arrival of the cheques, a bevy of snowmachines arrived from camps in every direction, and the money has long since been turned into groceries now being consumed out on the land. Today's holiday is a chance for the few remaining office and service workers to go out fishing or hunting for the day. Starting shortly after noon yesterday, one qamutik after another left, until now there is very little movement in the village.

There are some workmen at the Transient Centre who are delighted to work today at some astronomical salary: double time with double over-time after eight hours, or some such. Minutes are dollar signs which blind them to anything else in the North.

2 July

Anna is still at camp so Mimi has her job at the Transient Centre. Of the twelve patrons, seven eat early, so I am there at 6:00 A.M. This morning, in addition to the usual evening snack dishes and cups, the remains of dinner lay in state on the table — untouched. My disposition was the worst casualty as I scrambled around, clearing the table and washing dishes before I had enough cutlery and plates to reset the table. Later I saw Mimi in the store and she explained that she had not cleaned up after dinner because her seven-year-old had awakened her at 1:00 A.M. yesterday morning, just after she had gone to bed. He and his friends played noisily all night, despite her supplications to be quiet, and only went to bed towards noon. "I was so tired," she told me, "that I slept right through until this morning."

When Inuit have a good reason for not doing what would normally be expected, time is irrelevant. When you find out later that there was a sick child or other emergency, it is automatically right and fitting that the expected task should not have been performed. Whereas the white person would notify someone or send a replacement, the Inuk assumes that what you learn later will account for everything. It may also be another manifestation of the attitude that something in which you are not involved does not exist. Mark has a way of walking off for two weeks and leaving the Transient Centre to run itself in his absence. And, of course, it does! The guests empty the honey bag themselves, they leave notes stating when they came and left so that Mark can bill them later, the cooks shop for and carry food up to the Transient Centre. The only three-star rating we will ever get, I suspect, is for relaxed atmosphere. I've been in the North long enough to understand things that I hope I someday will be able to accept with magnanimity.

11 July

The plumbers have finished their work and are waiting for the plane. Some of them walked up to the cemetery yesterday and this morning want to know what "That white monstrosity that looks like a neon sign in church" might be. It is the Eastern Arctic Research Laboratory which most people refer to as "the mushroom" but which I see as a door knob. It blends into the winter white, but the men are right — it is eye-catching in the brown summer landscape. A couple of them, concerned about conservation of the Inuit way of life as well as the land, decided the anachronistic structure is a symbol of what should not happen. The plumbers think it stands as a warning to the Inuit not to accept indiscriminately whatever the white man offers. Some of the men here doing mineral exploration were not too impressed with the plumbers' observations. There are four geologists, a helicopter pilot, and an engineer in the exploration party, all recovering nicely from the food poisoning from which they were suffering when they arrived a few days go. If their Calgary boss approves, I will go with them to Arctic Bay as cook for two weeks.

There was a call on the radio this noon for a teen-ager to come in in time to get the plane tomorrow to go to Fort Smith for a mechanics' training course. There is also a group of four women, three men, and thirteen children ranging from one month to fourteen years, going to Toronto tomorrow. One tells me they will be there for six weeks demonstrating their art at an exhibit. They will do throat singing and drum dancing, carving between performances. "It will be hot," she frowns, "but we'll get lots of money," and she smiles.

19 July — Arctic Bay

For a while it looked as if we might have a Bastille Day happening. On July 14 the helicopter flew ahead with one of the men and the rest of us came by Twin Otter, leaving Igloolik at almost midnight. I nodded to the sun rolling along the horizon and went to sleep while the geologists and Arthur, the helicopter engineer, played cards. It may have been the tension in the cabin that wakened me for the men were talking softly, questioning Arthur, who was diagnosing the spluttering of the right engine. When it stopped he explained the mechanics of restarting it, speculating ruefully on the diminishing chances as it growled and gasped, growled and grasped without catching. As we flew on in the bright sunshine, the men discussed what gear to jettison if we started losing altitude. What had been a beautiful landscape of rugged plateaus scored by deep gorges and narrow fiords, now looked inhospitable if not downright threatening. As the men discussed the possibility of landing on a beach, I watched for the cross on an island around the point from Arctic Bay, but had not spotted it when the plane began to lose altitude. For the next few moments the tension in the cabin was palpable. I recognized the ridge of mountains to the east of Arctic Bay, and as the strip rose to meet us, the men went limp. Only later did I realize I was the only passenger who had landed there before. Since they were looking out the windows to the right and left, they could not see the village straight ahead, and were convinced we were making a forced landing. It's true, the tiny strip tucked in so close to the mountain does seem like an extension of the beach. Our landing had been so smooth and normal that I'd forgotten we were flying on only one engine.

Each day I pack lunches for the geologists, and, after a big breakfast, Andy, the helicopter pilot, drops them on the land. Eight hours later he picks them up at the end of their traverses, and when they get home we have our big meal. With the constant daylight, clock time doesn't matter, and each day we seem to lose an hour or two. Yesterday — or was it today? — we had our big meal at midnight and when I went to bed at 2:00 A.M., Arthur was still doing his maintenance on the machine. Today the men tried to get out early because they want to be back in time go to the dance tonight. I am washing their blue jeans so that they may be properly attired for the occasion.

It's a real pleasure for me to cook with such a variety of ingredients; at Igloolik at this time of year the choice of staples is limited, and the quality of what fresh food there is, is miserable compared to what we have here. The Calgary company rented a house here and ordered food from the South, flown in through Resolute Bay. In addition to the staples there are gorgeous meats, fresh fruits and vegetables, and such delicacies as yogurt, granola, nuts, and candies.

While the men are out on traverse, I have time to roam around visiting old friends and new and enjoying the sights of the village. I visit quite often with Sila and Toby at his sister's where they are staying. Tutu and Tommy are living with Tommy's parents, and Natika has gone to work at the mine in Nanisivik. Rebecca's English seems to have improved considerably, but that may be because she is older and less shy, and the children here seem to speak English among themselves, whereas in Igloolik they speak Inuktitut.

One day Rebecca, Suzie, their cousin Piuju and her two children and I walked through the pass behind the village, down the other side of the mountain to Victor Bay, looking for maktaaq that the girls had heard was there. Sure enough, we found a cache of igunaq, as well as abandoned tent sites full of interesting bits and pieces, junk and treasures. We poked along for five hours enjoying each other and everything along the way.

In Arctic Bay, an old woman has made herself a carving studio of sheets of construction plastic and canvas stretched on a frame in front of her house. Inside, a caribou mat, unfinished carvings, an array of tools, and the makings for tea look eerie through the rain-splattered plastic. She is snug in her lair, heated by a single-burner hot-plate plugged into an extension cord from the house.

Behind the last row of houses, the hill where seal skins are staked out to dry is littered with whale-bone chips and fragments of the beautiful grey-green soapstone streaked with white and brown that is associated with Arctic Bay carvings. My crew was agog at a narwhal tusk being used as a pole to launch and land a canoe. Nearby stands a white, wooden playpen resplendent with a caribou-skin-covered bottom. Stirred either by people or the wind, the playground equipment clinks and clanks an accompaniment to the laughter of play throughout both the days and the nights.

Day before yesterday I got to go to Strathcona Sound in the helicopter. The Nanisivik mine management had agreed to allow our people to use their big crane to hold up the machine while Arthur and Andy changed the pontoons for skids. While we were there the icebreaker *Sir John A. Macdonald* arrived with its Bell Jet Ranger helicopter just like ours. At least once a day it comes growling over from the mine site. On our way home, Andy cut loose with what Arthur told me was their special ride to dazzle the ladies. We raced along at 120 miles per hour just above the ground, up and down hill, over the cliff, then whirling in tight turns that pulled me first one way then the other. At one point I thought "How blue the water is!" then realized I was looking at Victor Bay through the blue-tinted glass in the roof over the pilot. I learned later that when he had burst over the cliff, Andy thought he was coming in over Arctic Bay, hence the detour and tight turns that I had enjoyed so much, while he found his way back through the correct pass to the settlement. I may have disappointed them by not squealing and giggling when Andy put the machine through its paces, but I can't remember a carnival ride I enjoyed more.

22 July

The geologists finished their work much faster than they had anticipated so I came home on the sched after just one week in Arctic Bay instead of two. The morning I left, with the blessing of the party chief I took boxes of oranges, celery, cabbages, marshmallows, and canned milk around to friends who were, of course, delighted. Now that I am home, I am exceedingly frustrated, as I was when I was delivering the goodie boxes at Arctic Bay, by my inability to communicate with the older Inuit who do not speak English. There is some kind of mental block that prevents me from learning Inuktitut. Maddening!

After being with people whose appreciation of the northern landscape is focused on its mineral content, and whose impression of village life is conditioned by its contrast to communities in southern

Canada, I more passionately appreciate the treasures of the beach and the whole naked settlement, stripped of its robe of snow. I *like* picking my way through bones and scraps of fur, skins and rusting motor tobbogan parts, loops of ujjuk thong hung to dry and old bits of it curled and knotted. I don't mind having my nose assaulted by rotting whale or seal carcasses or even by broken honey bags. How much more interesting than manicured lawns, pruned hedges, and paved streets!

When I thanked Sally for watering my plants while I was at Arctic Bay, I was surprised to learn it was her father Inaq who cared for them. These rugged hunters delight me with their gentleness towards children and, in this case, plants. I've developed a literal appreciation of the term *gentle-man* from living among hunters.

The ice went out of the bay on the eighteenth of July, the day before I got home and this morning a breeze off the water is sea-fresh. I can hear the waves on the beach but in less than an hour the floating ice will be wedged against the shore, changing the sound of the slapping waves.

The floor Inaq has laid for my porch is an ideal sundeck. I have an extension cord strung out the window, around the house to where I'm typing in the sun, laughing at a brown-and-white pup who tumbles back onto his black-and-white companions whenever my typewriter carriage shoots past his inquisitive nose. Some children have an imaginary tent between my house and my neighbour's. A little boy, seven or eight years old, is practising cracking a whip and I wonder if he will grow up knowing dog teams or only pooches. Are the little girls arranging pebbles and ivory chips into furniture for their play tent developing an artist's eye and co-ordination like their mums'? Will they too learn to cut and sew skin clothing for their families, or will they only care for manufactured items?

Siaku tells me "The birds are walking over there," gesturing towards the north shore of the island, and no doubt meaning that the newly hatched chicks cannot yet fly. I suspect that mine is the only house not filled with the chirping and squeaking of baby birds not yet able to fly.

The sky is pink around midnight, presaging the day when the dark will win back its way.

26 July

Burning refuse seems invariably to contain seal skins or fat whose odoriferous smoke disputes primacy with the acrid smell of broken honey bag wafted across the settlement. Except for the smells, an Inuit village during the summer reminds me of a tidal pool. On the peaceful surface, ever so slowly, swirl clusters of flotsam and jetsam; groups of children with a dog or a bike. As the clusters languidly glide with the water's listless motion, a unit or two may detach themselves and drift off, or a single unit/bubble may attach itself to the cluster.

27 July

This morning I arrived at the Transient Centre with bacon and eggs in mind, but there was no bacon. I shifted my plans to French toast, only to discover there was no bread either. The table was ready and the coffee was perking as, clad in my parka, I sallied down the hall towards the door, startling the first guest astir on his way to the bathroom. In Mark's house, four doors away, I threw open the freezer where I found Brussels sprouts, rolls of half-chewed ujjuk, French fries, a caribou leg, whole char, mixed vegetables, whale skin, caribou rump, broccoli, and. . . bacon. On my way back towards the kitchen with my prize, I smiled a greeting to the same patron emerging from the bathroom and busied myself fixing bacon and pancakes. The newcomers are two government employees from Yellowknife whose first question was, "Is it true that the Catholics live on one side of town and the Anglicans on the other?" "Of course," I replied and launched into my well rehearsed explanation of the phenomenon so often attributed to religious prejudice or fanaticism.

The extended family groupings so basic to camp life persist in a modified form in the settlement. Inuit like to have houses next door to their parents, siblings, and other relatives. The first families that came into the village from the camps chose to live by their pastors, and, since children are usually raised in the faith of their parents, the result in Igloolik is that each congregation lives grouped around its church. Chance, whimsy, or perhaps the Divine Sense of Humour has arranged the settlement with all common services housed in its centre: the schools, the RCMP buildings, the Nursing Station, Hudson's Bay Company, power plant, Transient Centre, and so on. On one side of these facilities lies the Anglican church compound with the parishioner's homes beyond it, and on the other side sits the large stone church and the Roman Catholic Mission. The conspicuous exceptions to this inadvertent city plan are the Co-operative, whose numerous buildings stand between the Catholic church property and the houses of the Catholics, and the Eastern Arctic Research Laboratory, high on the slope among the Anglican houses.

28 July

Today those Yellowknife men are a-twitter about our postal service which they categorize as non-service. Igloolik's mail is scheduled to arrive and depart twice a week, and it usually does . . . unless the weather is bad, the plane breaks down, the postmistress can't get the mail ready in time, there are so many passengers on the plane that there is no room for mail, the boys forget to take the mail to the airstrip, the waybills aren't ready when the plane is being loaded, or the bags are sent to the wrong settlement.

Post Office hours change with each new plane schedule. Most recently the Twin Otter from Hall Beach comes around noon to take passengers to the jet strip at that settlement, and it returns in the evening, bringing passengers from the jet. So on plane day the Post Office is open in the morning to prepare the outgoing mail. In the evening, when the incoming mail is sorted, a radio announcement tells people to pick it up within the hour — usually around 8:30 or 9:00 P.M., but perhaps as late as 11:00 P.M. or midnight. These days the postmistress carries the key with her and conducts business at any hour, for this is the season when hunters come in from camp to sell seal skins and carvings and to pick up pilot biscuits, Pampers, and chocolate bars to take back to their families. The postmistress tells me she has opened as many as five times in a day and at such odd hours as 5:00 A.M. The northern sun makes a mockery of day and night.

The pay is so low that the job is more of a hobby than gainful employment, which may explain why there has always been a mistress here and no master. The service is personal and unhurried. There are always volunteers to help sort the mail and distribute it to the children who frequent the Post Office. A typical exchange might be, "My uncle's mail too, and my grandfather's." "Your mother's father or your father's father?" with never a name mentioned. A young person may ask, "Did it come?" to be answered sadly, "Not this time," or someone else may be greeted with a jubilant, "It's here!" Catalogue orders are eagerly awaited by some, and, particularly in this settlement where every family has children and many have ten or more, the arrival of family allowance cheques is a happy event. During the summer their arrival is announced over the radio, and in the winter, rummage sales and bingos are timed to coincide with their availability, and the eternal patik games take on new vigour until the wealth is redistributed.

The Igloolik Post office operates somewhat like a substation of the Frobisher Bay Post Office. To procure a money order an Igloolik patron must send his money in an open envelope to the Frobisher Bay Post Office, whose clerk issues the money order, inserts it in the purchaser's envelope, and sends it on its way. COD parcels are held at the Frobisher Bay Post Office which notifies the Igloolik customer. When the money has been received in Frobisher Bay, the parcel is expedited. The northern phase of delivering a COD normally takes about three weeks but can be lengthened by bad flying weather and the numerous other factors which complicate northern transportation and communications. As neighbouring settlements acquire the responsibility for CODs and money orders the local populace is realizing that these time frames are not nationwide or even normal, but they nonetheless retain the attitude that a few days or weeks don't really matter enough to try to change the system.

To those who have trouble adapting to the North, the postal system is the umbilical cord to their mother culture. There can be some pathetically funny incidents when that cord is jostled. One night a full grown white woman, tears streaming down her face, slogged home from the house of the postmistress, also white, who refused to return to the Post Office after 10:30 P.M.

29 July

For once I was in the right place at the right time. After feeding my people Tuesday morning, I walked home from the Transient Centre along the beach — my favourite detour during most of the year. When I got home I took my camera and went right back to photograph the fresh seal draped over the deck of a fishing boat. Sauntering home, I came across Jeannie in her down parka, wool cloche, and wind-pants.

"Where are you going?"

"Out for narwhal."

"May I come along?"

"I don't know. Ask my husband. He went up to my Mum's house to get something he forgot." I could see Uinga striding past my house, crossing the street to Pigak's. By the time I reached my front door, my unbuttoned and unzipped clothes were dropping off like scales. I scrambled into long johns, blue jeans, extra T-shirt, sweat shirt, duffel socks, and rubber boots, grabbed the nearest wind-pants — down-filled for mid-winter — and an old, more than disreputable, down parka. Into the pockets I stuffed duffel mitts in their moose-hide covers and hand-knit Christmas-present gloves. Clutching my camera, a scarf, and hooded sweat shirt, I ran to the beach, ponytail swinging wildly — just as Uinga and Jeannie drew away from the shore! Their backs were to me and my cries were drowned out by the motor until they stopped at her adopted brother Joshua's boat. When they saw me I yelled, "Is there room for me?" Their canoe pulled back to shore, I hopped in, and by 9:00 A.M. we were under way.

"I didn't have time to bring anything," I told Jeannie meaning dried fruit, pilot biscuits, home-baked bread, hard candy, or anything else to add to the larder, or even my personal supplies and insurance against disaster; metal mug, extra film, lip pomade, extra socks, mitts, kerchief, or kamiks. As soon as we were well under way, her husband signalled for Jeannie to take the tiller while he blew up the seal-skin float. "You should learn to run a motor," she remarked. My attitude towards outboard motors is the same as towards motor toboggans. Since I'm not mechanically inclined I prefer to walk, or, in the case of boats, ride with someone else, rather than be stuck somewhere with a recalcitrant engine. "If you could run a motor well," Jeannie added, "you could be useful hunting." My attitude changed instantly.

"When I was young I ran motors," I volunteered, perhaps too eagerly.

"That's not enough," rejoined Jeannie. "You should learn again now that you are old." Meanwhile Uinga bounced on the half-inflated avataq for a while before announcing that it leaked too much.

We coasted to a standstill as Tukilaq drew up on one side of us and Atani on the other. Tukilaq's is one of the craft with a steering wheel rigged forward. Other hunters have improvised sprayboards at the bow, removable to allow for maximum speed when desired, and still others have built mini-cabins in their canoes to carry wives and families in comfort. The men were all exuberant, announcing, "We're going to eat maktaaq," lighting cigarettes and pipes, and pouring tea or coffee from Thermoses. They kept us company until Tukilaq had emptied the contents of a red plastic five-gallon container into his motor, then we all raced off, dodging among the ice cakes. What looked like slicks turned out to be films of new ice which crackled as we roared through it.

Though I had brought my camera, I was really out for beauty and experience and I found both. Snug in down clothing, with only my face poking out, I basked in the sun and drank in colours (blues, whites, browns, greens, greys with black accents); shapes (clouds, waves, ice, land, rocks); and movements (the canoe, water, clouds, other boats, whales, and, very rarely, a seal). Particularly fascinating were the rocks with their fantastically detailed banding, folding and fracturing intertwining reds, oranges, greenish-yellows, whites, greys, pinks, bright yellows, and, upon close inspection, even greens. Every now and then an icy blast on my face — like pinpricks — reminded me that I was still on earth and had not drifted off into some idyllic nether world.

We had lost our travelling companions in the ice floes but found them again in the sheltered, island-dotted waters of the recesses of Avvajja inlet. As we came through the pass between hilly land formations, scattered down the length of the waterway before us were eighteen or twenty boats of various descriptions. The smallest was a fibreglass dory a mere fifteen feet long, the largest a twenty-four-foot Lake Winnipeg fishing boat, but most were freighter canoes like ours, between eighteen and twenty-two feet long with outboard motors ranging from thirty to eighty-five horse power. All six of the village speed boats were there though the four whaleboats were missing. There was a bit of wind roughing up the water, making the whales difficult to see when they surfaced. As we cruised slowly about peering at the water, shots rang out, drawing all eyes to their source. It was Tukilaq on the hillside, gesturing, like a ballet dancer, with his whole body, arms imitating the graceful rolling of the whales, directing us towards a pod in the middle of the channel. As the hunters spied them, Tukilaq's dance became a frenzied "go-get-'em!" ending in a gleeful "I-can-almost-taste-'em" run down to his canoe.

Boats came and went all day and night, but there were always lots everywhere. Whale hunters wander at random, racing towards a pod when it breaks water. After a few shots the animals disappear, and the cruising, watching, and waiting begins again. More than once we had to stop before coming into someone's line of fire, and I was pleasantly surprised that no hunter was wounded in the crossfire. When a whale is shot, it is harpooned and left with a float attached to it. Some men used empty jerry-cans like the one Uinga had attached to his harpoon line. Far more picturesque, though not so colourful, were the rotund, sealskin avataqs, paws raised, bobbing daruma-like on the waves. If the float drags, or if the whale starts surfacing and diving, someone will dispatch the animal and usually help himself to a bit of maktaaq.

Several young traditionalists hunted with harpoons only, while others, including Uinga, did so only late in the chase, after running out of ammunition for their rifles. Once, just as Uinga raised his harpoon for the thrust, another boat came at the animals full speed, and their bow-man jabbed his harpoon home as our helmsman headed off to avoid being rammed by the intruder. The bumptious hunters who fired from impossible distances, causing the animals to dive and cutting off other hunters, seemed to take the most whales, which rankled my white man's sense of justice. But if it bothered the Inuit, they did not show it. Hunters close to a kill might later help themselves to generous portions after working only a short time skinning the animal they did not get to kill. Though we did not get a whale, we went home with plenty of meat from animals that Uinga helped process.

While meandering, watching for whales to surface, we pulled up to one dragging its float despite seven bullet holes in its back. After Uinga dispatched it with a carefully aimed shot from his .303 rifle, we paused for a nibble of flipper. The appendages, including the tail, are skin and gristle sandwiches without the layer of fat which underlies the rest of the skin. They are chewy and delicately flavoured. The gristle is impossible for me to pulverize with my dentures, but makes excellent chewing gum, tougher and of much longer lasting flavour than manufactured brands.

In mid-afternoon we pulled into a delightful bay where Tukilaq had hitched his canoe to the head of a tugaalik — tusked whale — and Pita was putting a line onto the tail. Like a streamlined plastic toy, the sleek cousin of the dolphin remained grounded on the shoal. Atani arrived and the three canoes managed to drag the ten- or twelve-foot-long animal to a pebbly beach, breaking the tusk and thereby greatly reducing its value, in the process. We had tea made when Toby's fishing boat pulled up and he and Angut added maktaaq and a flipper to our snack of square, hard pilot biscuits, the only non-whale food I'd had all day. When the men went to help the whale-skinners, I climbed up nearby cliffs, grazing on yellow kukilik flowers and sorrel as I went. In the distance multicoloured boats dotted the blue water, trailing white wakes like ribbons between the islands. Below me three men in hip-waders stood in the water slicing off skin while six men, sitting one behind the other on the rocks sloping up from the beach, held a steadying line around the carcass. When the men in the water had removed the accessible skin, those on shore hauled together, presenting an unskinned area towards the workers. A ten-year-old boy, the only child in the group, sometimes helped, sometimes ran errands, and sometimes slipped off like me to enjoy the land. When I got back to the beach the workers' Coleman stove had been set up and I joined Jeannie for a mug of tea. In front of us Tukilaq was chipping the tusk — the long eye tooth — away from the jaw bone with powerful axe blows. He tossed a piece of the small tusk that does not protrude beyond the skin to Jeannie. More welcome were the soft bones Jeannie favours and which I also enjoyed. The crunchy texture was nice and, as is the case with so many wild foods, the flavour delicate. Later, we all assembled at Tukilaq's summons to study a frothy white patch behind an eye, and my appetite vanished: close inspection revealed a writhing mass of tiny white worms.

A couple of times I noticed the working men's hands bleeding, but by the time the job was done, the healing properties of the fat had staunched the sometimes copious flow of blood. Jeannie produced a towel when Uinga had rinsed his hands with salt water, and the rest of the men lined up to wipe off the fat which is responsible for the soft hands of the hunters and of the women who flense skins. By the time we were ready to come home, using the towel saturated with the lanolin-like fat had become a beauty treatment.

Jeannie and her husband worked well as a team, alternating shooting and steering the boat. I added to the team effort by spotting the prey, sometimes before the other boats. I read all the instructions on the motor and observed how Annie and Uinga handled the craft hoping to try my hand, but every time I asked Jeannie if she'd like me to take the helm, my offer was refused. Now and then people would hold a couple of canoes together for a chat, and sometimes a man would change boats or go ashore for a while. Once a figure with a rifle over his shoulder hailed us from shore. It was Uinga's older brother, Timuti, who took over the hunter's position in the bow and was soon giving orders: "Slow down!", "Faster!", "Go over there," "Turn around," until he asked to be put back ashore.

"That's gold," Jeannie informed me, as we drew closer to shore, pointing out a slash of yellow that disappeared then reappeared farther along among the bands of rocks. "My husband's father brought some home." We landed close by to fill a water pan from a stranded patch of ice and I told Jeannie I'd like to get a piece of gold. "No," she retorted. "You'd tell people about it and we'd have a bunch of white men coming in digging up the land!"

We followed a pair of white whales for a while with no success then joined another party ashore, butchering their catch. Jeannie had set up our stove, put ice on to melt, and was about to get out the mugs and pilot biscuits when Timuti materialized from the group and decided to go back out hunting. As he tried to launch his brother's boat it stuck, so he called to a teen-ager to help him. We watched as the boat roared around and around quite fast, now and then gliding to a halt when the engine died. Like some impatient water bug with the hiccups, alternating stalling with bursts of speed, the skiff ran up and down the stretch of water in which we had all been hunting. A single animal surfaced ahead and to the left of the speeding canoe. When those on shore realized the hunters had not seen it they called and gestured, but to no avail; Timuti kept looking straight ahead and could not hear over the engine. When a pod surfaced close to shore, two canoes were launched from our party and Timuti joined them as they gave chase. However, he soon gave up and returned with our tea mugs.

My host took a large section of meat to feed the litter of seven pups he plans to raise into a team. When I asked if the Inuit ate the whale meat, Uinga replied, "Only if it is aged," and threw a couple of slabs of meat into the pile of maktaaq being buried under rocks to age.

A few hours later Jeannie was circling the canoe slowly, careful not to stir up the wind for her husband had lit the Primus stove and was brewing coffee in the boat. The couple had had very little sleep the previous night and were talking about going home when a canoe pulled alongside and in jumped Timuti. Relieved of the tiller, Jeannie — six months pregnant — lay down on an air mattress in the bottom of the boat and was asleep almost immediately. The new skipper dashed and swerved this way and that, almost blowing out the fire, then sent water swishing up out of the kettle with a lurch of the canoe as the engine died. Around 2 A.M. he decided we should go home.

We picked up some whale skin left ashore earlier in the day and stopped where Joshua was setting up a tent. He loaded his maktaaq into our boat and poured fuel into a can at Uinga's request, cautioning, "I only gave you two gallons." Uinga flopped down next to his wife and was also asleep in no time. After twenty minutes travelling at a steady speed back the way we had come in the morning, we met Inaq coming towards us. "Lots of whales," he called, gesturing behind him, in the direction we were headed. Beyond the next narrows were the twenty boats we had been racing around with twelve hours earlier, and, sure enough, whales soon surfaced not far from us. I edged back to the stern. "You shoot if you wish. I'll run the motor." Timuti's first reaction was a negative wrinkling of the nose, then — as if not daring to hope for such good fortune — "Can you run it?" he queried, and rose to let me take over. Presently I killed the engine and couldn't get it into neutral. Timuti came back and, after a struggle, moved the gear lever, started the engine, and returned to his lookout. We cruised a bit and chased a couple of pods along with the rest of the gang — then came our moment of glory. Before my hunter or the other vessels spotted them, I had spied two whales and raced towards them. I brought the craft in, slowing down precisely as the black-and-white backs humped up alongside. Alas, the shot missed.

After some more hunting I again killed the engine, set the gears and — on the third pull — engaged the motor, but turned to find Timuti had awakened Uinga and was coming to relieve me at the helm.

Several times the elder man announced, "Well, that's it," or "Let's head for home," and the younger man agreed, but each time, like a bridge player thinking the next hand will reveal that Grand Slam, we waited for just one more shot. When we did finally leave the other boats, I began to pray that we'd have enough fuel to get home. We turned down the inlet, passed a spectacular cliff full of nesting seagulls, drove by stretches of grotesquely patterned rocks, and eventually burst out from the lee of the islands. There we were confronted by masses of ice flashing bright white, pale blue, and startling emerald green against the navy blue wind-ruffled water.

The northwest wind was just cold enough to be uncomfortable, with my ears telling me they wouldn't put up with much more before making their displeasure felt, and sinus twinges accompanying the pulsing in my fingers and the numbness of those two once-frozen toes. But it was my rear end I became most aware of. I sat for a while on my customary thwart, feet up on the tucker box, until my back or side ached, then I'd let my feet dangle until the aches crept in again. Each time I shifted, I was aware of a bruised ridge where my bum pressed on the thwart.

We ran in the teeth of the northwest wind right into the mouth of Turton Bay, turned towards the settlement — and the motor coughed to a halt. I passed back a very lightweight fuel can from which Timuti extracted a cup of gas, and we prudently made our way along the comforting curve of the shore towards the village instead of straight through floating ice some distance from land. As the canoe rode up onto the gravel beach, I asked the time.

"Going on eight o'clock."

"Thank you," I answered and ran up the slope unbuttoning and unzipping. My clothes fell like autumn leaves as I dashed into my house, leapt into a pair of slacks and a shirt, combed only my bangs and scurried up to the Transient Centre, unkempt ponytail swinging wildly. Not a soul was there, though four men were supposed to have had breakfast at 7:30. I had tea made and the coffee perking when the first workman stumbled in. "Where's the rest of the gang?" I asked, as if I'd been waiting for them for ages. . . .

30 July

Inaq is often fussing with his camping gear or just gazing out the window at the water as I pass his house on my way to work. Yesterday, between breakfast and his arrival at my house, as I sat reading in the sun on the unfinished porch, sheltered from the northwest breeze, it was obvious why he never comes to hammer before 11:00 A.M. He would awaken the slumbering villagers. The rhythm of the village seems to follow a pattern. As in every milieu, there are dangers local residents learn to live with. The most obvious hazards for children here are the water and the tools of the hunter's trade — firearms, hooks, harpoons, and so on — which lie along the shore or in casual confusion around houses. However, children of six or seven, ten or twelve years of age prowl, undeterred, all night. The adults visit evenings until 1:00 or 2:00 A.M., then sleep until noon. Meanwhile the children come home and sleep until the afternoon, giving the parents the early afternoon hours free, so to speak. It's a nice rhythm, tenable here in view of the relative safety of the village, the weather, daylight, and, not least, the temperament of the people and their style of child-rearing.

When two or three families lived together in snow houses, the children (those that survived) were with adults almost constantly. A child started life watching its mother's work over her shoulder from its perch in the amauti. During the long cold months, whenever they played outside the pouch it was with their siblings or visiting children, quietly, behind the adults who were seated on the edge of the sleeping platform, sewing, making hunting tools, tending the lamp, or whatever. When the children played outdoors it was with toy harpoons and spears, bows and arrows, puppies hitched to tiny qamutiks. They imitated their elders and in play learned their life's work. If there were reasons to constrain a child, he was diverted from the danger he was courting. The youngster who reached for the flame of the qulliq was taken to breast or given a piece of chewed meat from the mouth of the father or mother; the toddler who staggered towards the summer shore or water hole in the lake ice was distracted by the gift of a feather, urged to nurse, or drawn away by some ruse of an older and wiser child. Children seldom heard the word for "no," and when they did, it was probably said as it is today — laughingly while the offender is cuddled so as not to implant the unhappy stress and confused guilt feelings which many other cultures instill into their young with a stern, unsmiling "no."

Traditional methods of training reflect several Inuit attitudes. One is the respect for the individual, but how much this is tied to the child's name is a moot question. Children were thought to have no "wisdom-spirit" (isuma) of their own until they reached the age of reason — about twelve or thirteen years. They were excused from what some would consider obedience because "they have no isuma. They do not understand." They were permitted what other societies might call selfish, egotisical behaviour "because they do not know," not because "they do not know better," but because they do not yet have the equipment with which to know. They were taught by example and the adults patiently waited until the growing spirit was strong enough to become the child's own isuma. Once the child had developed enough to be a responsible member of the community, he would be expected to learn through reacting to those around him, by an almost innate sensitivity to the desires of others, for though he was important, the survival of the group was everybody's first concern. The ratio of space per person in an Inuit camp of snow houses or skin tents compared to that in most North American multi-chambered houses, makes such an idea less preposterous than it first sounds to a southern reader.

But the respect shown the young child was actually respect for the spirit guiding him until his own spirit developed. Upon dying, an Inuk man or woman's spirit waited restlessly for another human home. When a baby was born, the waiting spirit was invited into it through the giving of the deceased's name. With the name and the spirit came the identity. If the name belonged to the father of the baby's mother, the baby was called "Father" by its mother, and was treated by the entire community as if it were its grandfather. The child *became* the "father" of its mother and was treated as such. You would respect your father's privacy if he did not wish to tell you where he had been. You wouldn't tell him, "It's time to go to bed." If your scraping of a seal skin annoyed your father, you would put it away until such time as he was not bothered by it.

With Christian baptism the Inuit acquired one more name and spirit, quite acceptable to a people glad of yet another spiritual protector. When the children go to school, perhaps to be enrolled under their Christian names, they usually maintain their name-spirit identity outside of school, in their families and in the total Inuit society. The boy whose teacher from Ontario may have made him write extra sentences for having disrupted class will come home to order his mother — who is the daughter of his name-spirit — to prepare his favourite food, or to give him money to buy candy bars and soda pop at the store.

What it took me years to realize is how prevalent some of these old attitudes are today. Taboos concerning social intercourse among in-laws, for instance, are still being observed today, not only among older relatives, but also among children bearing the names of relatives.

In the camps, caring for children was not exclusive to the child's parents but was shared by everyone. As early as they were able, they entered into adult activities. An older man here in Igloolik, upon returning from a camping trip one fall, told me with great pride that his grandson had shot his first caribou. The boy was four years old! Obviously an adult held the gun for him, aimed it, and helped him pull the trigger — but he shot the animal. He was becoming a hunter! One can imagine how, a hundred years ago, the grandfather would have walked through the hills slowly enough for the little lad to keep up with him, helping him pull his bow and fell his first caribou. Inuit children probably never heard the reply that so often frustrates children in other societies, "Wait until you are older."

The same camp people have been enticed by the government to

take up permanent residence in settlements which are growing to over a thousand people — huge conglomerations compared with the ten or twenty or forty members of a camp. There are many more children now than there were in the camp days, which means the adults spend less time with each child. The hostility of the environment has been tamed by the power plants which not only afford heat and light for the houses, but also lights for outdoors. The children are expected to spend several hours a day away from their families, attending school, and more and more men work at wage employment. After school young people may congregate in the stores or community hall. The houses are larger than the iglus of old and can accommodate a group of youngsters. Teen-agers can retire to a room away from the adults, possibly taking their baby sisters or brothers with them as in the old days, but not to learn the work their parents are doing. If the mother cannot sew enough kamiks for the whole family, there are boots for sale at the store. Recently, down-filled parkas have all but replaced the home-sewn duffel parkas, allowing the housewives to concentrate on the sewing of caribou-skin clothing for the hunters. Actually, southern residents can hunt with the Inuit using all southern clothing and equipment, items also available to the Inuk with money. The children no longer have to learn to make those things in order to assure their future survival.

Bring these elements together and you have the raw material for a social crisis in the North today. Children retain the identity of an adult, thus putting their behaviour beyond restraints; young people grow up in a society in which they do not have to learn skills from their parents; there are proportionately more young people than before in relation to adults, and there are also numerically many times more young people living in close proximity with each other; through the school and other contacts with white society, the young people learn cultural mores unknown to their parents, yet at home, they are, in some respects, treated quite traditionally. The elements are all there for an acute generation gap and it is only because there are mitigating factors in the Inuit traditions that persist, that the gap is not wider than it is.

I'm learning a bit about porch building as I try to help Inaq without getting in the way. Sometimes he assigns me a task, such as pulling nails, and sometimes we work as a team, he with the crowbar, I with my hammer. I enjoy the work.

The nurses are gathering large, flat stones from the hill towards the airstrip, building a patio and barbeque. They have more optimism or perhaps just warmer blood than I.

They had a bad day yesterday. In the morning, an Inuk brought in his four-year-old son who had been poked in the eye with a stitch remover. The nurses decided on medical evacuation, but all the planes based in Hall Beach were on flights resupplying the DEW-line. The weather was out, grounding aircraft at Resolute Bay, so when the sched came back to Frobisher Bay from Cape Dorset, they sent it here. There is an arrangement whereby patients are sent from all Baffin settlements for consultation with various Montreal medical specialists who spend a few days at the Frobisher Bay Hospital. During the six-hour wait for a plane, the nurses arranged to send two heart patients for Friday's clinic on the chartered aircraft instead of on today's scheduled flight. This time a nurse was not needed to escort the little patient since the mother, with her baby in the amauti, went with her son.

31 July

After the narwhal hunt, when the feasting was over and the spate of hunting tales abated, the people realized Igloolik had exceeded the federal Fisheries and Oceans Division narwhal quota for the settlement. Replete residents had consumed thirty-six animals instead of the twenty-five allotted to them.

Through the Federal Fisheries Act, Parliament has given the responsibility for inland waters and oceans to federal game management personnel who may enact protective regulations for fish — legally defined as any living inhabitant of the waters other than plants. In 1975 and 1976 narwhal quotas were determined for each Inuit settlement. The quotas were arrived at by studying past kill statistics and by estimating the total narwhal population in each area as well as the whales' reproductive rate. A figure called the "sustainable yield" — the number of animals that may be taken without depleting the population — was reached. Arctic Bay and Pond Inlet, the area where the small whales are most concentrated, were allowed one hundred animals each year. Only ten, fifteen, or twenty were assigned to hunters in areas of incidental populations where few animals had previously been killed, such as Broughton Island, Clyde River, and Pangnirtung on the east coast of Baffin Island, and Hall Beach and Igloolik on Foxe Basin to the west of Baffin Island.

In an effort to counter the local complaint that laws are made in the south, local Hunters' and Trappers' Associations have been given various responsibilities, and their members have been invited to work with government field officers furnishing data on habits and availability of game as well as harvest statistics. The numbered, metal tags allotted for species for which quotas are imposed by the government, are distributed by the local HTAs. In some settlements the Inuit have chosen to draw for them. In Igloolik the economic needs of each hunter are assessed and their game already taken reviewed before deciding who will receive tags for bear, walrus, whales, and caribou for sale rather than for home consumption.

In the eastern Arctic, there has been definite co-operation between the Inuit HTAs and wildlife management personnel on both the territorial and federal levels. The people have provided information about numbers of animals, migration routes, and calving areas, supplementing technical information such as thickness of fat layers and age statistics gathered by scientists.

Igloolik had twice before exceeded its quota for narwhal. During freeze-up in 1979, the regional federal game law enforcement officer in Frobisher Bay received a phone call from Igloolik informing him that a pod of approximately 105 narwhal was trapped by ice and shallow water at Agu Bay, north of Igloolik. The hunters were allowed to legally harvest the naturally doomed animals in a well organized (and photographed!) community hunt. Consequently, as soon as they found they had exceeded their quota a second time in August, 1980, it was with the confidence of being fairly treated that the Igloolik Hunter's and Trappers' Association went on the air over CBII to call for a moratorium on narwhal hunting until federal fisheries representatives could come for consultation.

During the ensuing talks, the hunters argued that, through a misassumption that they were taking animals from the small Repulse Bay population to the south, their quota had been set too low. Since they are actually harvesting from the large, healthy herd that winters in the Davis Strait off the coast of Greenland and summers in north Baffin, they felt they should be allowed fifty tags. A temporary compromise figure of twenty-five was reached only after the HTA had unsuccessfully tried to phone the Federal Fisheries and Oceans Minister in Ottawa. The local federal fisheries officer feared that the initiative of appealing directly to the cabinet minister might indicate a belief that the legislation of northern fisheries offices was not to be taken seriously. On the other hand, he was glad to have Inuit call the attention of the powers in Ottawa to the lack of funds for research and information-gathering necessary for the efficient, equitable management of game in the north.

The Inuit feeling towards this type of management of their most precious natural resource — game — was perhaps best expressed by the chairman of the Pond Inlet Hunters' and Trappers' Association, meeting with legislators from Ottawa in the North for the first time. "We are glad to see you visiting the North," he said, "because if we had to make laws for Ottawa, we would certainly visit the south."

August

1 August

When I dressed to go fix breakfast at the Transient Centre this morning, I put on long johns and a heavy turtleneck shirt under my lady-like clothes. By eight o'clock I had fed my people and hurried over to Toby's house to see if he really would let me go along walrus hunting. He was pacing, drinking tea.

"Shall I bring my sleeping bag?" I greeted him.

He grinned. "No. I'm not going to sleep." Then he asked, "Is the tide high?"

"The boat is half in the water," I replied, and scurried home without further ado to don the warm hunting clothes I had dug out the day before, and to stuff a loaf of homemade bread, a jar of instant coffee, a pound of dried prunes, and my tea mug into a sack with a change of boots, stockings, mitts, and kerchief.

By 9:00 A.M. Angut, Toby, Abraham, and I were heading out of Turton Bay in the sturdy Lake Winnipeg fishing boat. Clouds wafted by a light southwest breeze were beginning to obscure the sun when the skipper, in high spirits, announced, "There's lots of water!"

"True," I thought, "considering the size of Foxe Basin, let alone Hudson Bay."

As we nudged up to a huge ice pan, Abraham hopped onto it with the anchor, followed by Angut carrying the water billy and an ujjuk harpoon line and I realized the remark referred to *fresh* water. After soaking the rope and stowing the drinking water, the hunters took aim at a small target of floating ice, adjusting and readjusting their rifles until they were satisfied they would aim true, then we proceeded out into Foxe Basin. As the helmsman threaded his way through slabs of ice whose dirty surfaces indicated walrus had been there, his partner worked the wet harpoon line over his foot, chewing the stiffer spots, before coiling the softened thong.

After about an hour, a change in the pitch of the motor as the skipper throttled down woke me. There ahead, to windward, was a clump of walrus on a small chunk of ice. We were only about fifty feet away when the first tusked head poked above the mass of bodies, butting the air inquisitively in our direction. The gesture was repeated by one or another of the eight animals until we were a mere twenty feet away and Angut's shot rang out. Grunting, the huge beasts flopped into the water one after another as the rifle cracked a second time. The animals flailed around near their ice pan, surfacing as a group, bobbing for a minute or two, snuffling and peering this way and that. Snorting, then rolling over each other, their backs breaking the water, they dove, only to reappear close by a few moments later. A brownish streak spreading in the water around the milling herd assured us that the bullets had hit their mark. Toby grabbed the metal harpoon shaft from the back of the craft, uncoiled the sealskin line, strung the harpoon, then dug in the tucker box. While the wounded walrus lagged behind its companions, the hunter — affecting a nonchalant pose — carefully filed the cutting edge of the harpoon head, then swiftly attached the red plastic jerry-can whose contents his partner had just emptied into the fuel tank. As Angut drew the boat alongside their whoofling prey, Toby thrust the harpoon home. The creature rose up, splashing the water into a white wreath around its immense head, and twirled several times before sinking below the surface, dragging the gyrating red float behind it. After several minutes of thrashing and whirling, we watched the red container slowly fade into the dark recesses of the icy water as the walrus sank for the last time. After a pause Toby shrugged, remarked matter-of-factly, "That was my only harpoon head," and once more we set off through the field of ice.

We were not long in sighting more of the mammals. Indeed, there seemed to be clumps of walrus all around us. We sidled up to a group of four, and as Toby's shot rang out, three of them scrambled into the water and the fourth — a large bull — rolled over on its back. The hunter shot again. The animal gave one last, tremendous heave and slipped into the water. "*Quyana* (Too bad)," Toby muttered.

As I scanned the heaps of walrus crowded on their floating perches, I amused myself by making up reasons why they squeezed themselves one against the other on pieces of ice just large enough to accommodate them, when larger chunks of ice were all around them. Whatever the reason, it made it harder for hunters in our predicament to bring home meat. As we approached the next pan, the dark ruck composed itself into mounded bodies from which rounded heads poked up for a moment or two, then sank back into the pile of odoriferous game. Three perfectly placed bullets produced as many lumps of meat and put to rout most of the surrounding animals. "Take a picture! Take a picture!" shouted the men as a mother and her calf remained on the ice. The calf wanted to nurse. The mother squinted at us with her tiny red eyes, then butted the youngster towards the water. But the little fellow — whose stomach ruled his reflexes — repeatedly waddled back to suckle. When the female finally managed to push her little one into the sea and rolled in after it, we approached the dead animals: a brown-haired female, a black-skinned, hairless male calf, and a full-grown male, flecked grey and black, underhair worn away along its massive wrinkles. The huge webbed flippers were also hairless, and at the ends of the four finger bones, well back from the edges of the appendages, were toenails, much shorter than those of a bearded seal. The nails and eyes are the only things small about these impressive creatures!

The men sharpened their butcher knives as they surveyed the two tons of meat they were about to carve for the dinner table. Each man slit an animal up the back and across the neck, then stood back as the blood arched in thin streams like some red waterworks display. While the large animals bled, the men cleaved the small walrus down the back, rolled it over, opened the belly, and loosened the intestines — not yet developed enough to be tasty — with one expert cut and pushed them into the sea. Next the head was severed and the flipper bones and backbone excised with lightning slashes of the frequently sharpened knives. One more stroke through the remaining layer of tissue and the meat lay in two neat portions, ready for the attentions of their wives.

The butchering of the adults was much the same, but entailed the co-operation of young Abraham with the meat hook, and even of me to manhandle the bulks before the backbones were disposed of. The heavy flipper bones were also discarded, but the penis bone — a favourite tourist trophy — would be sold to the Co-op. While Toby prepared meat to be rolled, Angut carefully squeezed the contents of the intestines into the water, and braided the emptied tubing, which he added to the pile of delicacies: a heart, a liver, and the skin and meat from the outside edge of the front flippers in to the finger bones. With an axe and his knife, he then cut out the upper jaws with their prized twin tusks and smaller teeth in between. He removed the tusks, but when a few bangs failed to loosen the teeth from the lower jaw, he muttered, "*Ajurnaqtuq* (It is difficult)," and went back to helping his partner process the mammoth carcasses. I appropriated the hatchet and had chipped one of the teeth before I discovered the trick of extracting them. Well-placed blows on the jawbone below the roots will pop the teeth out, but in order to place the blows properly I had to cut away tongue and lip. Though walrus teeth have a rounded root instead of the branched roots of many mammals, they are nonetheless firmly set.

The meat and hide, freed from the ribs, was cut into eight or ten large slabs, punctured with rows of parallel slits on all four sides. A strip of hide fashioned into a long rope was used to lace the segments of meat in the neat rolls I'd admired arriving in the settlement after hunts. The fat of the walrus is layered in the meat rather than lying under the skin in a single, insulating stratum as in most northern mammals. This layering produces a striped, interlarded effect when the rolls are served after having been aged into the igunaq for which Igloolik is famous.

The flippers were packaged by cutting thong lacing from the body end of the hide, then folding the flipper in upon the meat and threading the thong through slits on two sides. After the laces are tied on each chunk of meat, a notched piece of hide or edge of rear flipper is inserted like a dowel rod to keep the slippery knot from unravelling. As I tied the knot on a piece I had just laced and was about to insert the safety plug, Angut materialized at my elbow offering me a notched morsel and retrieving the delicacy I had mistaken for an expendable bit. Wrestling with the jiggling, unruly masses kept me warm and busy while I amused myself observing the textures of the fat, meat, hide, and salt-water ice-slush clinging to the lacing strips.

During the four hours it took the Inuit to prepare the bounty, more herds of the sea mammals drifted by. When the men were loading the meat from our floating workbench into the boat, I suddenly realized something was missing. "No stomach?" I asked. "Yes. No stomach," came the reply. I tried to hide my disappointment. In the excitement of really being there, watching everything happening, I'd forgotten what I'd thought of as the best reason for being at the kill of a walrus: to be one of the few to savour the delicious contents of the stomach —

tender clams marinated in digestive juices. We all munched on flipper while working, and once I was delegated to make tea, but, because of the threatening weather the men did not take time out to feast and chat as they usually do on a successful hunt.

It had been misting and raining while the hunters worked, and as we headed for home the sky was filled with black clouds, in some areas blending into a solid curtain of grey. Sunlight shone like a single spotlight in the distance, below the clouds, and though there was not much wind, huge swells broke into white caps, rolling the heavily laden craft despite its broad beam. Angut, the only smoker on board, became master of the camp stove with his lighter, presiding at tea-making. As we climbed the swells and wallowed in their troughs, Angut filled the fuel tank, dismantled the pump, rubbed the leather gasket on a loop of walrus fat oozing over the braiding, reassembled the plunger, and proceeded to brew up a mug. During the long hours of fighting the high running seas, I favoured a perch standing on a side bench, head above the cockpit canopy, nose in the wind. Every now and then I would come in for tea or another dried prune or two, then resume my stance. Once I stepped back onto the handle of the meat hook, slipped, ricochetted off the walrus onto the fiberglass engine cover, banging my temple with a resounding thwack, and bounced back onto my feet with a grin for the three worried expressions peering at me. I kept forgetting the fall until I tried to open my mouth to stuff in another prune, or to take off my glasses, and yawning was painful for days. Small damage considering what might have happened!

One hour, another, then another — and I began to wonder just where Igloolik might be. Finally Angut turned to me and called out "*Uglirlarjuk,*" indicating a dark shadow barely discernible against the greyness of cloud and light rain in which we had been swathed. For another hour, we followed the coast as the rain abated, and in the grey twilight came upon five white tents at Kangiq. It was 10:00 P.M.

We visited in the tents, two on one side of the small river and three on the other. About a hundred yards upstream, the river bed suddenly changed from pebbles to slabs of rock rising in a series of waterfalls at fifteen- to twenty-yard intervals. The terrain was pale grey gravel and rocks with here and there a hollow spread with moss and tiny tundra plants flaunting a few yellow and white blossoms but mostly going to seed in splashes of orange, red, yellow, and brown. Piles of excrement, multicoloured toilet tissue, and disposable diapers were everywhere, adding colour if not allure.

When our party reassembled, the boat was pulled parallel to the shore and Toby tossed the rolled meat into the shallow water. When it had been hauled above the high-water mark, the hunter drew himself up to his full height, surveyed the surrounding area, gestured with his head and announced, "Up there." Shouts summoned the rest of the men and more children. The men lined up, those in the middle grasping a roll in each hand, and off they went — four huge sausages sagging between the five men, climbing heavy-footed up the gravel incline to a large pit. Most of the children could not even budge the meat — nor could I for that matter — but two of the larger boys struggled manfully up the slope bending under the weight of the smallest parcel.

When the fifteen or more packs of meat were assembled, Toby threw them — as if they were hollow! — into the depression, then aligned them neatly. I wondered why none of the observers gathered around the pit moved to help. When the last of the meat was positioned to his satisfaction, the hunter placed a few flat rocks onto the bits of meat exposed along the lacing slits. When he started covering the hides with gravel, the men who had been leaning on shovels joined in, and Toby passed his tool to another man. The Inuit took turns with the three shovels hoisting the heavy pebbles onto the growing mound; the children added their bit using toys or their hands. When the men seemed to consider the job done, Toby started again, this time throwing showers of gravel in great arcs over the neatly levelled edges of the hill onto the hump of hides in the middle. The other men followed his lead and bent into the task. I thought the men's muscles must surely be quivering from fatigue! After a while, Toby, followed by several children, climbed onto the cache. It joggled under his rocking motions so he continued piling gravel onto the meat. A second time the movement under his feet was slight enough for him to consider the cache adequate and he strode off towards the shore.

It was half past midnight when we arrived at the beach in Igloolik where Arnak, Sita, and an assortment of children greeted us. "We saw you a long way out," said the wives. More people arrived as the ribs, heart, flippers, and other delicacies were unloaded. Though I knew I would miss the ritual retelling of the day's events and the general festive atmosphere of homecoming, instead of repairing to a hunter's house I trudged off up the beach to my house. A young couple chatted with me outdoors by my water tank as I ran water into my washtub to rinse the salt water off my outer layer of clothing. It was 2:00 A.M. by the time I had bathed, washed my clothes, and crawled into bed, tired but delighted that after ten years of begging I'd finally got to go on a walrus hunt.

4 August

My garden is doing beautifully. The dwarf marigolds are a delight, an orange seed has sprouted, a melon plant is sending out tendrils to support its large leaves, the philodendron and airplane plant slips look as if they'll survive, the nasturtium flaunts one emaciated bud, and leaf by leaf my visitors and I have been enjoying the lettuce and chard.

A couple of children of friends have developed a taste for the wheat sprouts I promote instead of candies. My favourite remains alfalfa sprouts, which I particularly fancy with seal liver. The last time I baked bread I added some sprouted mung beans to one loaf and some soaked but not sprouted wheat seeds to another. Sita, my gourmet taster, found the mung concoction edible but not exceptional, and she carefully picked out the wheat seeds, which I considered crunchy and she diagnosed as hazardous. At least she found no graphic epithet for them as she had for a previous caraway loaf!

Southerners wince when they pay 50¢ each for pears, 55¢ each for apples, 70¢ each for oranges, and $1.38 each for grapefruit; or $2.30 for a head of lettuce, $3.42 for two pounds of carrots, and $6.50 for five pounds of potatoes, but most of them balk at paying between $2 and $3 a loaf for more-than-a-day-old and often mashed-in-transit bread. Prices that stifle the appetites of those raised elsewhere are normal to local Inuit. A woman cooking in the south may plan her menus then go shopping to purchase the items listed. A northern cook will go to the store and plan her meals around what is available. If she learned to cook in the south, here she learns to substitute, extrapolate, invent, and experiment. These cooks are neither squeamish nor timid, for they have learned to confront and dominate strange raw materials. It is unsafe to leave any indiscriminate animal or vegetable matter in the kitchens of this breed, for their reflexes are such that they instinctively regard the unknown as a challenge — which the head of the house will probably meet on his dinner plate.

My distraction during Mass today was a comparative analysis of Anglican and Catholic church services. Eight-, ten-, or twelve-year-old Catholic girls, who arrive with younger brother or sister tucked into their little amautis as toys, squeeze in among the wriggling mass of children in the front rows. During the service there is a constant movement: toddlers are chased, babies are hauled from child to child to mother to aunt to grandmother and back again. Six- and eight-year-old boys and girls fuss over two- and three-year-olds, goading them when not playing with them. Mothers drag children out of amautis to fondle them, evoking gurgles that eventually turn into howling complaints.

Action at the altar proceeds to the rhythm of shuffle, rustle, murmur, scuffle, punctuated by bursts of loud child and baby noises. Music to the ears of Inuit? I wonder what profound religious beliefs are expressed through the action in churches. What inner state lies beneath the chaos? For me it is an excellent school for faith and true prayer.

Some things about the Anglican service create a more reverent atmosphere for me: the measured pace during the reading of prayers, the long pause after "Amen's" when everyone remains silent, heads bowed. As a rule, the mothers keep the babies and do not allow the children to play or run in and out of church as is customary at the Catholic church. More children of all ages sit with their Anglican parents, reducing the numbers of front-row squirmers. The toddlers lurching in the aisle and howling babies appear as exceptions in the Anglican congregation, rather than the rule. When women cannot quiet babies, they take them out — under disapproving stares. Catholic missionaries tell me the people feel more at ease in their church because the Anglicans imposed the European behaviour code along with Christian dogma, so when I find it easier to pray in the Anglican gathering, it may just be my cultural predisposition again colouring my judgements and reactions. Inuit have always lived more or less comfortably with spirits depending on who the spirit was. My distractive musings ended in a chuckle as I slipped my fellow God-Spirit worshippers in with the Italians in the adage: "For Americans the church is 'the House of God'; for the French it is 'la maison du Père'; for Italians it is 'la casa di papa.'"

5 August

These are beautiful summer days — northern summer, with temperatures around 5° and 10° C, sometimes zooming up to 15°, rarely 20°, and at other times dropping below zero, turning rain into snow. Some days fog lies softly on the land until devoured by the sun's rays or eased on by gentle breezes. On other days clouds drop their rain or snow on us in their haste to evade the winds. The tide scratches its path on the glassy surface of the sea, etching ripple lines that parallel the shore from the far end of the settlement, then suddenly swinging away at right angles to the beach. The fickle tide, laughing at ice chunks, runs away while its erstwhile playmates, unable to follow, lie weeping on the beach. The returning tide finds the ragged ice configurations smaller and sadder, still dripping tears.

6 August

A government land-use inspector is spending a few days in Igloolik. His host is the local Game Management Officer: his job is to inspect camps of holders of land-use permits, for example, Geological Survey of Canada teams, mineral company exploration crews. As the inspector explained, "I told them in the camps that I wasn't there to get on their backs but to see that they were disposing of their wastes properly and respecting the regulations, so that if later the Eskimos complain they left a messy site or damaged the land, I can testify on their behalf.

"Eskimos must kill fewer walrus," he declared. "The herds are declining." To the question "How are you going to prove to the Inuit that the herds have diminished?" he replied, "We're just going to have to tell them they can shoot so many and no more. They're leaving lots of meat and taking only the tusks and penis bones." The suggestion that the hunters needed the trophy money for fuel, ammunition, and hunting equipment fell on deaf ears. "I've been taking pictures," the official snapped, "Just wait until Eskimos come into my office with their stories about living in harmony with the animals and the land. . . ."

Today, ecstatic after a day of fishing, he listed the various animals he had seen and photographed. "Even a killer whale! But I won't say where," he added, "or the Eskimos will go out and kill it!"

8 August

That elusive Greenland whale (not a killer whale!) spotted in the area for four out of the last five years, has again challenged the hunters to the thrill of the chase. The feverish activity along the beach was echoed by discussions over the radio.

An elder phoned in to say, "Game Management Officers have arrived in our settlements. We are told more and more often not to kill this or that animal. Quotas have been imposed on walrus and polar bear and caribou meat is now sold when bearing the proper government tag. The government people would probably not want us to kill the whale." Then he reminded listeners of the last public meetings with some oil and mineral exploration company executives. With land-use permits in hand, they had come to consult with the people. "Will you cancel your exploration plans if we ask you to do so?" asked the Inuit.

"No," replied the executives. "The federal government has issued us land-use permits and you do not have the power to rescind them. We are merely telling you what we are going to do."

"For years," the elder on the radio ruminated, "we have been telling the government people we don't want drilling in northern waters or blasting and digging on the land to scare or hurt the animals. The government will not listen to us when we speak about the land and the animals. Why should we listen to them when they make laws about the land and the animals? We should kill the whale and enjoy maktak if we can."

10 August

On the spur of the moment this morning, I went out in Inaq's canoe with Inaq, his twelve-year-old son Johnny, and Eli. The intensity of the pale blues and aquas of the sculptured ice was accentuated by the proximity of white snow and deep blue water. Each piece of floating ice is an exquisite masterpiece fashioned by the lapping waters. It bobs in the waves and rolls as the sun whittles away a weak spot. Peaks of clear, glistening ice or still snow-whitened surfaces surround pools of water nestling in basins hollowed out by the waves and sun. In the bright light they flaunt the same gaudy blue-green as a swimming pool in Hollywood or Beverly Hills. A variety of clouds were scattered around the baby blue sky; under a bank of black-tipped clouds the same sky became a dirty, smoggy yellow.

We pulled the boat up on shore and set a net at the mouth of a river. While tea water heated and overhead jaegers wheeled and dove at us, the men shot at a tiny piece of ice for target practice. When each wandered off his own way, I walked along the river, finding brown and white mushrooms and bringing back a tiny fern. It started to rain as the men pulled in the net containing one fish and a kanajuq (sea sculpin) which to me looks more like a practical joke than a fish.

Twice we stopped in the misty rain to thread our way through floating ice. We spotted a pair of akpak (which my dictionary says is a kind of penguin), so Inaq stalked them with the boat, starting slowly towards them, finally racing at them as one dove and the other took off into the air. Inaq performed all afternoon. When he stopped to scan the ice or while running the canoe, he would sing ai-yi songs and bounce the craft along in rhythm with his singing by pumping the throttle. We spied a seal but missed it. Near Igloolik Point we came across Toby and Angut who were seal hunting. We chatted with them a moment, and when their prey surfaced we all shot at it. No one got it though, so we headed for home. Soon we caught up with Kinakiar and Tali and their family in a whaleboat. Again we all chased and missed their seal, then raced them home with Inaq clowning around with the motor. A couple of times he cut the engine quickly, almost toppling Eli from his perch on the thwart. Close to shore was a canoe just setting out, so we made a sharp turn and ran towards them, crossing their wake just astern of them at full speed, then we headed back for shore. It was a lovely, fun day full of simple pleasures.

Tonight around midnight, there was a full moon casting real moon-light for the first time since spring.

15 August

Inaq has finished the porch and now that it is closed in I miss spending the beautiful mornings in the open, reading in the sun, sheltered from the wind. The deck I've built is smaller and the sun is no longer so warm, but maybe it will be inviting next summer. I am a mass of cuts and bruises, but I think my carpentry work is done for a while. Having finished off the new and inner porches with hooks, nails and a shelf, I attacked the inside. I painted and installed moulding around the floor, caulked the wind and rain cracks around the windows, and put skirting around the porch, all in an effort to cut the draughts and help my poor little stove in its battle against the cold. Maybe this winter I won't have to live with my feet in the stove.

Siaku and Toby came by for coffee this morning. Toby picked up the string on my table and started making figures. The old man took his turn and soon the men were engrossed, relaxing and enjoying themselves. They taught each other figures and vied with each other though never, through gesture or word, belittling one another. Each never "saw" the mistakes made by the other as they learned new figures. Thus, when Siaku was teaching Toby "the walrus head," he would do two or three figures, then "the walrus head," then another figure or two and give the string to Toby. Toby would then do a figure or two, try "the walrus head," which he would not be able to finish, do another figure and return the string to Siaku who would start over. Siaku would never stop Toby when he made a mistake, but let him observe and learn by himself from watching the figure correctly performed.

Perhaps the other side of this Inuit habit of not calling attention to another's mistakes is the idea that an Inuk is never wrong. Not quite as appealing a trait if you are trying to teach or complete a new type of project for the first time. There seem to be no correct or incorrect ways of doing things but rather "your way" and "my way" — "the white man's way" and "the Inuit way."

16 August

There is a huge, fluffy baby snowy owl waddling around in the dust in front of the house next door. Inuit love anything tiny and cuddly: babies, puppies, birds. The former are always in season, but only at this time of year are there baby birds to love to death.

19 August

I have celebrated this, the first day of school, by cooking breakfast then buying groceries for the Transient Centre. Next I cleaned a former teacher's house so that another teacher could move into it. Finally I packed — too fast, for the things I forgot to bring make a longer list than those I have with me — and at 5:00 P.M. left by canoe with Joshua, Uinga, Jeannie, and their daughters Louise and Jolly. Two hours later we landed at Nirlirnaqtuq and added our tents to a row of three dotting the gravel around a small cove. While I was prowling around visiting in various tents, Uinga's younger brother Davidee and older brother Timuti drove the bow of their canoe onto the beach and tossed a cut-up ujjuk overboard. While Davidee dragged the meat up the beach, I watched Timuti skin two seals. I almost held my breath for fear he'd slit the precious skins with his huge, swift slashes. I need not have worried, for his deft strokes bespoke the poetry of a master at work. Attracted by the silvery appearance of the last hunks of meat Davidee was hauling, I drew closer and discovered they were covered with glistening sea lice rolling off like shining drops of oil.

20 August

I was the first one to stir, gathering flat rocks during low tide and making a patio in front of my tent. The small children were up next, extracting yips from a litter of pups. Later, visiting with two women as they flensed seal skins, I learned that the men were out caribou hunting. After a while one of the women casually asked, "Aren't you going with Uinga?" and I noticed their tent was down. In a flash I packed, struck my tent, and joined them in the canoe.

The wind that had driven rain squalls against my tent during the night now assaulted us as we tried to get through the ice to Baffin Island. Sometimes in the lee of a large bank of ice the water was calm, but as soon as we got through, there would be waves. One scene struck me as being like the New Mexico desert, blue water in the foreground substituting for the yellow-reds of sand and sage. In the distance were purple and blue hills; near at hand, yellow, brown, and grey hills. Rocky, rocky! Threading through narrow passages between islands or among ice blocks, twisting this way and that . . . what appeared to be shallows turning out to be currents swift enough to ruffle the water. In spite of Uinga's efforts, my outer layer of clothing was soaked, but, happily, waterproof enough that I was not overly uncomfortable: just the usual cold hands and feet despite the ten- or fifteen-degree air temperature.

We stopped fairly often, climbing onto the floating ice to make coffee and to reconnoitre, trying to plot a course through the floes. The men finally changed their goal from Baffin to some smaller island where they had seen caribou during the winter. We caught two seals and at a stop on an island, saw lots of loon and a few duck eggs. The girls brought along a baby loon, too young to fly, but when we camped, they forgot it in the canoe. We passed Naujaaruluk — a cliff face covered with seagulls — but we usually see more jaegers, flocks of ducks, and some snow geese. In the water are several varieties of jelly fish and other small things I cannot identify. It was windy all day and all night. In my tent I fried seal liver in seal fat for everyone and enjoyed boiled seal and broth with rice in the other tent. It is almost dark at night now.

21 August

The movement of the canoe, at the end of a long rope at low tide reminds me of a horse on a tether. In slow motion she runs to the end of the slack, then her head jerks back, she rears a bit and runs off the other way until once more checked by the end of the line. It is the still-strong north wind blowing her. But in the lee, on one of my walks today, it was warm enough to flop down on the heather, in my five layers of clothing, point my nose at the sun, and nap for half an hour until I woke myself snoring. As the men left in the boat, Uinga said they would sleep when they return and when they awake we will move camp.

22 August

We set out in a north wind at about 3:00 P.M. When someone would call out "Natiq" we would hope to get the seal, and we did take a small one among the ice blocks. For a long time I hesitated, finally calling out "Umiarjuak." On the horizon, amid the floes, was a white ship that we later learned was the Baffinland. We followed her helicopter to a small island where some of the men met us as we landed. They spoke with Uinga and Joshua, who speaks excellent English, while I kept in the background, speaking only to Jeannie in Inuktitut. We managed to pass me off as an Inuk. Our prank succeeded so well that one of the men even asked Joshua if we were all of his family. They took pictures of us and gave Jolly a sack of cookies from their orange storage shed. They were erecting navigational aid towers, placing bench markers, and putting out tide gauges, and they told us that instead of burning the shed and another like it on Jens Munk Island as prescribed by environmental regulations, they would leave them for the men to pick up after October. Later we found a bench mark which the Inuit thought would be taken out by higher fall tides. At the bottom of a cove we also found a complicated rig, like a trap, with a cable and rope to a box that I assumed contained instruments, swathed in canvas and covered with rocks.

We spent the day in the canoe prowling around the water and

islands. The rocks were endlessly fascinating: reds, browns, whites, pinks, and greys, banded, streaked, striated, folded, and sheared. We came close to several seagull nesting cliffs and the Inuit spotted a falcon nest high up a cliff. We put Joshua ashore and watched from the boat as he tried unsuccessfuly to reach the nest. There was a full moon around 11:00 P.M., pink above a curtain of rose and mauve drawn between the deep blue of the water and pale blue of the sky.

23 August

Today was the first day without a strong north wind. In the early afternoon the men took Louise seal hunting and I went mountain climbing, following waterfalls up to their sources. Near the cliff full of gulls, it was like visiting a cathedral. The crevasses were side chapels, one all green, another sun-washed red and green. There was milky, pale green stone by the water's edge, then cliffs of red angles and shadows. As I walked among the huge boulders, there were threads of water everywhere, sometimes falling, sometimes flowing or spurting, and in one place, throbbing rhythmically. One cascade tirelessly rolled out perfect crystal beads, tossing them one by one over a red cliff to form a stream below. As I prowled and climbed, the sounds of the water changed constantly from splashing to gurgling, laughing to singing — sounds bursting forth in some places, receding in others, as the water groped its way under the rough piles of huge boulders. We played hide-and-seek for a long time, the water and I!

The hunters returned, reported high waves to the southeast, deposited Louise and a seal, ate, and went off again. Later they brought back another seal and once more set out. This time they rushed right back to herald fish at the mouth of the river. Alas, no one had brought fishing tackle. We all scrambled around, poking in the debris left by previous campers. Joshua fashioned a spear with an old piece of wood and a knife; Uinga made a spinner from a spoon; Jeannie and I knotted shreds and tatters of what had been a large net into a small net, and we were off! Joshua, Jeannie, and I set our net while Uinga went farther around the cove and cast his spinner to no avail. Then Jeannie and I watched from shore while the girls pointed out fish, Uinga guided the craft, and Joshua stood in the bow thrusting his spear. It had started to sprinkle as we arrived at the river mouth and by the time we had reconciled ourselves to doing without fresh fish, it was raining quite hard. I was glad to warm up and dry out while I cooked a bedtime snack of pancakes in my tent. During the night the noise of a party pitching camp awakened me but did not lure me out to welcome them. It was Davidee and Timuti on the way home after a successful beluga hunt.

24 August

Patches of rain and rough seas kept the boats beached today. Most of the time everyone was content to stay in the tents visiting, napping, and eating raw or boiled maktaaq, which I found a welcome change from seal.

Louise is nine years old. Jolly, who is seven, still has her bottle from time to time. During a conversation among Uinga, Jeannie, and Joshua, Jolly was demanding her mother's constant attention and, of course, being indulged. Jeannie was interested and participating in the conversation. While one of the others spoke to her she talked with the child but answered the adults right away. If I, with my qallunaaq reactions, had been Joshua or Uinga, I would have been annoyed or felt slighted that Jeannie was not patently paying attention to what I was saying since she was occupied with the child. The scenario suddenly reminded me of a church service. The woman's behaviour was the same as that of mothers during Mass, perpetually soothing, indulging, obeying the children, tossing off a response or an amen on cue. It seems most unprayerful to me, but I'm a childless qallunaaq. . . .

25 August

It was still windy and rainy today as we packed up and left for home, watching for game along the way. Several times we had to argue right of way with grounded ice near the shores of islands, sometimes backing the boat out as the tide withdrew, threatening to strand us as well as the ice. A couple of times we all got out and walked in shallow water, pulling the loaded canoe until it could once again float easily. Once we got caught in the midst of grounded ice, our escape route blocked by a low arch connecting two icy goliaths. Uinga took out his rifle and put three well aimed rounds into the arch, which collapsed, allowing us free passage. Later, amid jumbled floes, we spotted an ujjuk disappearing and reappearing somewhat like the mist, which folded us in grey dampness one minute only to sweep off, clearing our vision, the next. Joshua shot it and tried to get a harpoon into the huge beast while Uinga brought the skiff up close. The seal disappeared under some ice, but we were close behind when it surfaced on the other side. We all scanned the water and ice around us for several tense, quiet moments, broken by cries of "*tavva*" when someone sighted our quarry. Then, without warning, the stillness was rent by a thump as the canoe was heaved out of the water. Instinctively all six of us thrust our weight towards the high gunwale and the craft flopped unsteadily into equilibrium as the enormous animal sank back into the water. Nobody said a word and the watch continued until our prey eluded us in the ice field. It was still windy when we pulled onto the beach at Igloolik in the wet, grey dawn.

September

Gulls screaming, dogs howling, laughs and calls of children, distant in the twilight; the slap, slap of the aerial, windblown against the corner of the house, and the ticking of my alarm clock: lovely night sounds of Igloolik.

1 September

The last summer Sunday at Nalaqqajarvik dawns clear and calm. The rising sun turns the frost on the white tent into grey, wet patches, and silver droplets fall from night-whitened guy ropes. Sila pulls herself over the edge of the igliq and, still lying on her stomach, pumps the camp stove, lights it, puts the kettle on, scootches back under the quilts, and puts Larry to her breast. Beside her, Sita squirms in his sleep. Toby soothes his son, pulls a quilt over Abraham's protruding feet and, in a few minutes, props himself up on one elbow to enjoy the mug of instant coffee with two heaping teaspoons of sugar prepared by his wife. His cup emptied, the Inuk pulls on his clothes, dons his kamiks and goes out. The older children pour themselves tea or coffee into which they dunk pilot biscuits, broken in half so they will fit into the mugs. Larry alternates between his bottle of diluted canned milk and his mother's breast while Sita dances among the prone bodies of his brothers and sisters, laughing and dripping milk on them from his bottle. As Sila finishes changing the little one and brushing the crumbs out of the bedding, Toby, who has been checking his net, returns with a four-pound char. The still drowsy children are thoroughly awakened by the prospect of fresh raw fish and from the caribou skins and mattresses watch every swipe of Sila's round-bladed ulu as she fillets the fish. The pieces disappear as fast as she piles them on a plate. Two of the diners wrestle for the bones until Toby settles the issue by giving each some to suck. After more sweet tea and pilot biscuits, the children are ready to play along the shore and exercise their marksmanship by throwing rocks at the red-legged sandpipers, terns, and passing loons.

3 September

When the sun shines, its glow is reflected by the dry, transparent leaves of one particular species of tiny plant, and the land shimmers. About three weeks ago I brought in some moss and tucked one of those plants in with it. While the tightly stretched membranes of the leaves of this plant have turned from white to palest gold outdoors, in my house the plant is putting out green shoots and preparing white blossoms. My door shimmers with the land. The new porch hinges are still shiny silver. With the silver tape patching a hole in the door, they make a lopsided triangle visible from across the settlement.

The reason Sila and Toby have not yet moved into their new house is that the whole domino arrangement broke down. One couple refused to move when they heard how much their new rent would be. The family who should move into their house was offered another which they refused because it was not near their relatives, and so on. These housing assignments become incredibly complicated because Inuit want to live near their parents, sisters and brothers, uncles and aunts or cousins. When one family moves, there are four or five others who also wish to change houses. It is no wonder the Housing Association Board of Directors meets night after night for hour upon hour to finalize assignments, only to have the whole scheme nullified by a single family's retraction!

Sila and Toby's present house will be given to Sila's sister Dora and her husband Simagak, who will move here from Repulse Bay. I remember him much better than his wife, for he was the local court jester, always laughing and causing laughter, though I couldn't understand what he said so was never sure why. When he walked in late and grinning, to a meeting of the Repulse Bay Settlement Council, of which he was an elected member, everyone burst out laughing even though he had not said a word. He's that sort — jolly, jaunty, likeable. I've forgotten their children's names, but no matter, for they are bound to have added several during the years since I've seen them.

8 September

Yesterday, with a sore throat, full head, aching ribs and bones, I rushed around in the gentle rain shopping, packing, and hauling stuff down to the beach in case there would be room in Atani's boat going to Agu Bay. There wasn't. With the boat gone and my exertion over, I took an antihistamine and went to bed.

The longliner *Apak* will travel with Kinakiar's whaleboat as he takes house material to the outpost camp at Ikpikitturjuaq, then hunts caribou on the return trip. Toby, who, as chairman of the Hunters' and Trappers' Committee is the skipper, says I may go along!

9 September

The ice and the first sealift ship came in with a southeast wind. By evening high tide, the barge and tug were immobilized, wedged against the side of the ship by ever-increasing ice. Once a year ships load in southern ports and, escorted by ice-breakers, wend their way north to Inuit settlements which are icebound all but two or three months of the year. Even in government literature, the popular designation "sealift" has finally replaced the pompous official title of "annual Arctic resupply."

Not too many years ago, during sealift stevedores roamed the streets asking small boys, "Do you have an older sister?" A few cigarettes or a candy bar usually turned muteness into smiles as the child led the man home. Other ship men approached groups of women carving outdoors, between the houses, paying fifty cents for miniature seals or seagulls. In Repulse Bay, the Bay manager used to close the store when the first ship arrived, opening for a couple of hours when the crews were safely aboard for the night. A Co-op clerk felt sorry for the stevedore so poor he had pocketed a pair of gloves without paying for them. During the winter a clerk in the Bay store opened a huge crate to find it half empty and upon close inspection found where it had been neatly slit and then reclosed. Soft drinks and various foods were always missing, for the crews had weeks on board with nothing to do between ports but inspect and sample the cargo.

In those days the ship's helicopter buzzed the settlement before landing amidst a crowd of curious adults as well as youngsters, and the ship's officers gallantly swept all white women — teachers, nurses, and even unaccompanied wives — into the bug for sightseeing flights, followed by dinner at the Captain's table. Today men are flown home from various northern ports after they have worked the number of days allowed by the unions, so female company is no longer at such a premium. Nor is there the constant traffic of small crafts between the ship and shore as Inuit visit on board, buying candy, tobacco, and gum, drinking coffee in the wardroom and selling carvings, skins, artifacts, and puppies.

I first observed sealift from one of the southern terminals — Churchill, Manitoba — where freight arrived by train and was stacked dockside awaiting transhipment to the villages around Hudson Bay. There I watched one of the priests of the Roman Catholic Mission water pallet-loads of squeaking, stinking chicks on their way to the Grey Nuns' egg factory at Chesterfield Inlet, and laughed at the children playing tag among the towering stacks of merchandise.

The first sealift I saw at the destination was unique. For some forgotten reason, the goods for the Co-op instead of being packed on pallets were merely tossed, case after case, into the lighter. Every child in town, according to his or her size, carried cans one by one or by the armload from the shuttle ship to the warehouse. All that year unlabelled cans, recovered from the barge bilge, were sold to the adventurous.

Exemplifying the old-time sealift fever was an incident when the first ship arrived one year during a high wind. Though the crews were waiting before venturing onto the water in small boats, two young Inuit lads prevailed upon a companion to take them in his canoe to the ship "for soda pop." When the craft capsized the ship's helicopter plucked the two young men from the rough sea. The canoe's owner, however, was never seen again.

The stores would be out of some items for weeks before the arrival of the ships. One year we had no paper: no paper towels, tissues, toilet paper, paper napkins, diapers — nothing!

Today the Inuit are sophisticated catalogue shoppers, however, sealift freight rates are still the lowest available to northern residents. Government employees from the south save considerably by ordering on sealift yearly. For several years the territorial government ran intensive education campaigns throughout the Northwest Territories explaining the system and advantages to Inuit and aiding them to place orders. Very few Inuit had the ready cash to profit from the procedure, but those who did, did so only once. With their year's supply arrived their relatives from surrounding villages. Two or three months later, when the provisions were gone, the relatives returned home. Some young Inuit today still feel bound to share purchased goods with relatives as was customary in pre-salary days. Though air freight is still very expensive, Iniut have money and will pay to have goods flown in or willingly pay the big store price reflecting air freight charges. Even so, there is still a rustle of excitement as the pile of goods on the beach is spirited away to warehouses from whence it filters onto the sparsely stocked store shelves.

An amazing number of parents used to visit the school when the government icebreaker arrived with huge tubs of ice cream for the children, and the only movies in the settlements were those brought by the ships and shown on their projectors in the Community Hall or the largest classroom, but the goodwill function of the ships has evaporated into business efficiency as the Inuit have progressed from the threshold of a mercantile economy to the fully furnished, soft centre of a consumer society.

12 September

The large tanker *Maple Branch*, small tanker, *Eider*, and cargo ship *Eskimo* are again surrounded by ice, unable to get the rest of their loads to shore until the ice shifts. The icebreaker *Wolfe* has come to resupply the *Eider*, so there are four ships in the harbour and a pesky little helicopter overhead. The *Apak* slipped through most of the ice and is moored to the east. Presumptuous little bit bobbing saucily at the four real ships. Other years, ice stranded by low tide has temporarily stopped unloading or there has been a crust of ice on the bay through which the tug had to break a path for each trip of the lighter. On one windy day, eight or ten twenty-foot canoes broke loose from the tugboat and drifted like a huge bunch of coconuts in their straw and burlap wrappings, among the floes. It took manoeuvring during several tides to lasso the wayward cluster.

Until now there have been few trucks in Igloolik; the water and fuel tank trucks, a couple of pickups owned by the Co-op and another belonging to the government of the Northwest Territories. This sealift has brought in a whole fleet of trucks: one each for the RCMP, the Hudson's Bay store, and the Northern Canada Power Commission, several for the Co-op and government, some for the Housing Association, and the hamlet, and a magnificent panel truck — a veritable car! — for the federal government's Eastern Arctic Research Laboratory. The ground is frozen with a light cover of hard snow, and all day and late into the nights trucks whizz around and around, criss-crossing the eight or ten streets in the village, then running the three kilometres to the airstrip and back. I suppose the euphoria will eventually be congealed by the descending mercury and disappearing sun and the hamlet will settle into a new way of life where the truck replaces two snowmachines as the local status symbol.

When unloading does proceed, everything is running smoothly. The cranes and fork-lifts were put ashore by the first barge. The tugboat pulls the loaded lighters from the hip, backs them into position at the beach, and the cranes and fork-lifts take over. On the mother ship, huge deck cranes swing pallets from the hold, over the side onto the waiting barge, which the tug will tow away. On the settlement side of the operation, scores of young people (one wonders why they are not in school) toss cases from the pallets onto truck beds, while adults watch, smiling. The Co-op fork-lift bounces merrily through town towards the latest construction site, one crate daintily balanced in its maw. Small children swarm over the piles of construction materials, conduit, barrels, and crates while others play hide-and-seek. On the steps of the Hudson's Bay store, shoppers pause to survey the scene, exchange gossip, and speculate on what the crates contain.

The ship men still prowl the stores looking for bargains and the local teen-agers still gather in goggling groups, but the electricity of a once-a-year occurrence is no longer there. These are just another bunch of white men among the many who now visit the settlements throughout the year.

16 September

Sila phoned to ask if I wanted some liver. When I got to their house I discovered that Simagak and his family had arrived from Repulse Bay. He is as gay and bouncy as ever, and his wife Dora, with her quiet smile, provides a good foil for his ebullience. I greeted them in the utility room where they were eating caribou with Toby and some children, then joined Sila at the table in the living room. While drinking tea and eating bannock, I watched Sita chasing Elizabeth — Simagak's five-year-old — who was chasing Larry while Simagak's twelve-year-old Eric and Ivo seemed to be playing a game using Abraham for the ball. "My liver?" I asked Toby as he dressed to go back to work. "Your liver" — he mimicked my error instead of saying "the caribou liver" — is outside in the tucker box on the qamutik," then he grinned, grabbing at me in the area where "my liver" should be. As I leaped back I landed on Sila's foot and turned to find her handing me a plastic bag, laughing at her husband's horse-play.

17 September

I am again struck by the unity of life here. What alarm I would cause Mother if I wrote, "I'm going on a sea voyage with the man who delivers water, the man who pumps fuel, a brain-damage case, and an occasional labourer." Yet here such men are capable land (and sea) men. A man's value is independent of his job rather than indicated by it; thus the mayor of the hamlet can be the school janitor. Our lives in western civilization are compartmentalized; those of the Inuit integrated. We can go to work and spend time with people who have no idea how we live. We are evaluated according to the job we perform. But in a settlement, even during this time of transition, a person's entire life, not just their job performance, will determine how they are regarded by those around them. So it doesn't matter what job you do, which in turn encourages people to try any job. I think over half the men in this village can drive the water truck, the fuel truck, collect the garbage, work in the Co-op, build houses, etc.; in other words, fill all but the clerical jobs. The traditional life in which each family unit had to be able to survive alone, encouraged such job mobility. But clerical work requires new skills and the Inuit seem to be bringing their cultural values or evaluations with them. Since only a few can fill these jobs there is an elitism inherent in them — at least in the eyes of the incumbent, which means in the eyes of the younger generation. And another thread in the traditional fabric snaps!

When the wind stopped and the men started loading lumber onto the longliner and whaleboat, I packed my things, dressed, and spent most of the day sitting on, or pacing near the beach. In the evening when my duffel bag went on board, I began to believe I really was going to get to go on the expedition! But the men went home.

18 September

The men worked all this morning on the longliner engine and, at 2:00 P.M. we finally set out. On board the whaleboat are Simagak, Atani and fourteen-year-old Elijah. With me on the *Apak* are Natika, Pita, and Toby. We saw the Hudson's Bay Company supply ship in the distance heading for the bay we had just left, and later we sighted a Greenland whale. I was surprised at how calmly the men viewed the whale, then realized that their reaction was that of serious men who were not free to pursue the animal, no matter how much they would have liked to. Their mission was to deliver building materials and bring in clothing skins and meat for the entire village.

Once beyond Turton Bay, the spray froze in icicles along the cabin rail and the deck was covered in mushy ice. Usually I slept on the shore in the tent with four of the men, and the skipper and one man slept aboard the longliner. The first night my tent-mates were Atani, Pita, Natika, and Elijah, who admired my down mummy bag. Atani crowned his inspection by announcing that henceforth he would sleep in it with me, then hooted with laughter. Inuit men are always teasing . . . and always available, for they can't understand a woman who prefers to live alone. Love radiates from families where babies are adored, children loved, and parenting is a pleasure as well as a duty. Since sex is an appetite comparable to eating or sleeping and a proposition usually no more than a friendly gesture, my "thanks but no thanks" reaction is accepted with a laugh or a shrug.

19 September

Though we arrived at Tunit's camp at 6:00 P.M. the men did not accept tea from their hosts before unloading the lumber and prefab house panels. When we could no longer help, the children gave me an escorted tour of the "matchbox" house, cleaned and being readied for winter occupancy, and of two old winter residences, which held the same fascination for me that abandoned houses always have. Discoloured sheets of plastic, newspapers, and scraps of fabric hung from the walls. Raised platforms divided the working/sleeping area from the storage area as is typical of Inuit dwellings, be they of snow, skin, or nowadays, canvas. In the litter were discarded wick-trimming instruments, parts of camp stoves and lanterns, toys, clothing, and scraps of paper and cardboard. The floors were as uninviting as any other abandoned Inuit camp or garbage dump.

A team of ten dogs was tethered some distance from the tents and close by was a drying rack with meat hanging high above my head. In one of the tents seal meat simmered over a stone lantern while an

Inuk — using the heavy vise, weight, and tools belonging to someone in the camp — worked steadily, whittling and filing a metal piece for the engine of the whaleboat. In the second tent the ladies served me tea from a kettle over another qulliq. When I admired their abundant meat supply, they showed me more of their wealth — an ample store of seal and whale fat to feed the lanterns whose low flame was sufficient to maintain the comfortable warmth that had greeted us when we stepped from the cold into the cosy canvas tent. For my benefit, the women performed the qulliq lighting ritual, pounding fat for the round-sided well of the vessel, then, along the straight edge of the soapstone basin, fashioning a wick from arctic cotton, gathered the previous fall before the plants had gone to seed. The facility with which they manipulated the burning wick to maintain a smoke-free flame belied the difficulty of the manoeuvre. Behind the tents, pebbles slid by the children on the new ice already covering half the lake sang a vibrant, squeaky melody until silenced by the water. The men finished their work in the dark, ate maktaaq and dried, frozen caribou, visited briefly, then retired to the *Apak* where we all slept in the empty hold.

20 September

In the morning we followed the shore south, threading our way through patches of fog, playing "I Spy" with the whaleboat among the islands and ice. At the mouth of a river, the parent ships stood offshore while their small boats set out to fill containers with river water. Once beyond the lee of the islands, we left the fog and plunged into an expanse of floating ice.

For hours I sat on the wheelhouse roof marvelling at the beauty of the glassy sea filled with chunks of ice, each a work of art. Each ice sculpture was mirrored on the sea, like so many Rorschach blots. The predominant colours were snow-white, the tan and brown of sand, black of seaweed, and the green and blue of the ice. Touches of yellow, hints of red, and striations created by layers of snow, tides, and sand, were bent and swirled then cast back arched and rolled by the watery reflection in our wake. Sometimes candled ice formed columns and pools. Other chunks were friction sculptures. There was an abundance of crockerips and snakodiles and a myriad more dragons and animals the names of which I have forgotten or never knew. Hour after hour they remained fascinating, though the barrier which kept us from our destination.

Not so comfortable was Natika's perch high up the mast. One arm wrapped around the spar he peered about, shielding his eyes and pointing out passages through the moving ice. Swinging down from his eyrie, he hung over me as if to land, feigned surprise at finding me underfoot, then laughingly dropped down next to me.

Travelling with the Inuit I am reminded of the good humour, love of fun, and camaraderie of the Japanese. Serious and demanding situations in which most westerners would react with tension, irritation, anger, or impatience bring laughter and clowning, though not incompetence. During hours of threading our way back and forth through the ice, there seemed to be no change of atmosphere, not even when we finally headed back the way we had come. The poor villagers and farmers that I met in Japan, rather than rebel against the hard life they accepted as inevitable, seized every opportunity to escape into laughter. Though Inuit used to live on the edge of survival, they sang about their hardships when their bellies were full.

In mid-afternoon we climbed to the highest point of a small island, hoping to see a lead through the ice jam. When we came upon a family of ducks swimming on a pond, one of the men was compelled — like any small boy — to put them to flight by tossing a rock at them. Later there must have been a thousand ducks like a cloud of mosquitoes rising and falling, sweeping over the water then circling near us to pass in review. And there were terns to watch, using their tails as well as their wings to perform graceful aerial acrobatics.

21 September

We once again spent the day travelling through ice, but instead of being compacted into obstacles, the huge pans — some larger than the islands we were passing — were being swept along individually by the currents and tides.

Pita sat on the hold hatch, his spyglass braced on his knee, scrutinizing the passing islands. He asked to be put ashore on one, and we watched him become a small speck ascending rocky cliffs. We continued to the far end of the island where we came into a cove almost encircled by a rocky spit. Just beyond the sand shore on the far side of the little bay grazed four caribou. As we anchored the *Apak* and went ashore in the canoe, they moved inland, grazing warily among the boulders. In the time it took me to find a small lake and return with a kettle full of water, Natika and Toby had shot and skinned the four animals and were butchering them. As they were hauling the meat to a gravel patch, Pita came trudging up, put aside the gun slung across his shoulders, and helped pile up the meat then cover it with rocks. Someone crowned the monument with an antlered head, and the men gathered for tea. Only then did Pita say that he had cached a caribou not far from where we had put him ashore.

Instead of going back to the longliner, Toby steered the canoe towards a smaller island a few hundred yards from the one we were leaving. He veered off from his set course as we sighted a bull walrus also heading for the island. The men watched the swimmer while keeping a sharp lookout for additional animals. As we obliquely neared our destination, we spotted a female on the far side of the bull, and we relaxed as the pair swam away from us.

We climbed to the ridge along the centre of the island from which the men checked the sea and sky conditions and I marvelled at the flowers still in bloom despite the fall frost. It looked as if the plants had gone to seed, preparing for winter, then the recent warm weather had induced them to bloom again. There were clumps of the tiniest daisies I have ever seen, perhaps not so surprising, since this is the farthest north I've ever seen daisies.

Later we passed another walrus riding in splendid isolation on his private ice raft, blissfully unaware of our passage until the men roused him from his reverie by barking. They lined the rail and set up a clamour worthy of a herd, causing the animal to rise up and stretch near-sightedly this way and that. The men continued the racket until the huge beast finally waddled to the edge of his sanctuary and slipped into the water. Then the men collapsed in laughter. He did look comical, swinging his great head in confusion, possibly wondering if he were still dreaming or really in danger. Maybe he dove into the icy water to clear his head.

By evening we had reached Qarmartalik, where Simagak, Atani, and Elijah had already brought their gear ashore from the whaleboat. When the tent had been raised Toby busied himself on the boat; Natika and Atani slung their rifles over their shoulders and purposefully strode past a small lake, away from the shore; Pita, spyglass bobbing jauntily from his back pocket, wandered over the ridge behind the tent out of sight; Elijah helped Simagak; I tried to make myself useful without getting in the way. Elijah and Simagak scooped gravel into a raised platform across the rear half of the tent floor area. On this they spread foam mattresses and caribou skins, carefully flattening and tucking, laying and relaying the materials until they had fashioned a smooth, level surface onto which they tossed each person's bedroll. The Coleman stove and lantern, water billy, cooking pots, various boxes and bags, and chunks of meat which I passed into the tent were arranged in their customary places, while the red plastic container of naphtha stood sentinel outside.

Caribou meat and tongues simmered on one burner and the kettle was about to boil on the other when Atani and Natika returned. The latter sniffed, searched in the food boxes, then stirred a package of dried chicken noodle soup mix into the meat pot. He had no sooner finished his contribution to the cuisine than Toby entered with ice gathered on his way to shore. He emptied the lake water from the kettle and put the ice on to heat while the hunters took off their boots and stretched out on the caribou skins. Elijah too slipped off his boots, sliding back to make room for Pita.

The conversation was desultory for some time while we busied ourselves stripping red muscle and chewy sinew from caribou legs. When picked clean, the bones were braced on a rock and split with a sharp blow from a knife handle. At this time of year both the fat and marrow are solid, pure white, and delicious. Though Inuit hunters wear bright plaid shirts or illustrated and lettered T-shirts instead of togas, and quaff tea, not wine as they lounge on their caribou skins after an evening meal, the relaxed conviviality that reigns in tent or snow-house seldom fails to remind me of the laurel-crowned Romans pictured in my old Latin grammar, lolling around their banquet benches.

After the feast, while the men exchanged minutiae of the days adventures over tea, Simagak sighed, "I'm homesick. Not for my wife," he added in English, "for my little girl." As if to console himself, he put water on to heat then rummaged in his packsack. First he produced a radio-cassette with which he fiddled until it blared forth American commercials interspersed with bursts of "music" that I feared might split the surrounding rocks as well as our eardrums. Next he poked around in the jumble of food, cooking implements, and tools on the ground in front of him until he found a small basin. Finally, from his rucksack, he brought out sweet-smelling soap and a towel, with which he carefully wiped out the basin before pouring in warm water to wash his hands and face. As he towelled his face dry, Natika picked up the soap, washed, and passed the basin on to Atani, who in turn performed his ablutions and passed the implements on to his left. By the time the now-cold, greasy water had been emptied, Simagak had drawn another treasure from the depths of the rucksack. Ear-splitting rock was replaced by side-splitting Charlie Panagoniak, recorded live at Frobisher Bay's Toonik Tyme celebration by the Inuk from whom Simagak had purchased the machine. The 45 rpm album recorded for the CBC some years before by the pride of Eskimo Point, is good but barely scratches the surface of Panagoniak's abilities as a performer. His interaction with the audience, particularly in the comic numbers, is enchanting. The hunters listened to the cassette over and over again until they knew every word and performed along with the artist and audience.

22 September

This sabbath is indeed a day of rest. Though someone makes tea from time to time, nobody will cook. People wander off for long walks, take their ease in the tent, nap or eat at will, alone, in pairs, or groups, when occupations and inclinations coincide. The Anglicans, who had brought their prayer books in calico drawstring pouches, read from them or sang as the spirit moved.

Once Natika stretched out on his back on the igliq, held his hymnal above his head, and started to sing. Toby scootched over next to him, laid his head against the singer's, and sang along. Pita entered, cocked his head and listened, smiling, then produced his song book too. Another time we all happened to converge on the tent simultaneously. Each had brought his thirst but no energy with which to slake it, so we devised a contest to determine who would make tea. We sat at the top of the hill in front of our camp and took turns throwing rocks at a pebble placed on a boulder below us. A player who knocked the pebble off replaced it then retired from competition. To the tune of much twitting and chaffing, Atani — the last person to knock the pebble off the boulder — put the kettle on. As we waited I toyed with a pebble, catching it in the branch of a piece of caribou antler. The Inuit recognized a game when they saw one and soon excelled me in my pastime.

It is cold with no wind to speak of, yet the movement of the ice has reversed directions. Without wave noise, it is so quiet that the distant sounds of bird calls and ice rumblings take on a phantom quality. Our footsteps in the coarse gravel are downright raucous, but the sound and sight of a huge chunk of ice breaking off or shifting is magnificent. I am intrigued with how drastically the shoreline changes with the hours and spend much time roaming over the low-tide landscape then retreating to the tent to warm my feet.

When we are all together Elijah is a model young Inuk, jumping to shore to haul up the canoe, filling the stove tank or water billy, silently carrying loads, ceding his seat — unbidden — on the igliq to perch among the boxes of meat, serving himself tea last, listening quietly while the men swap tales in the evening, and crouching in the back of the tent to bed down last wherever there is room left. But today, when there were only the three of us in the tent, he went berserk, bedevilling Pita unmercifully, questioning him, demanding answers instead of Pita's usual gentle smile, snatching off his cap and putting it on him front to back as often as Pita would rearrange the cap. Another time, he peered in and seeing me alone in the tent, burst in demanding to know what I was writing and tried to seize my papers. Delightful one minute; a demon possessed the next!

Yesterday, as I searched along the shore for a spot from which to fill the water bucket, Natika called "Come here," and I realized he was standing on the lake, dipping in his container from the edge of ice so clear I hadn't realized the lake was half frozen. Today the entire surface is frozen and we chip a hole through which to draw water. The marshes and tundra will be hard frozen underfoot for the hunt.

I had no sooner finished dining on raw caribou shoulder than Pita came along and I watched him finish off a head. The front muzzle had been slit lengthwise. He knew exactly where to poke in a finger or knife point, or crack with the knife blade to get at every bit of tastiness. The eyes, prominent delicacies, had long since disappeared, but there were bits of muscle, cartilage, and sinew to be had. I watched mesmerized as Pita sliced off the outer layer of the back molar and ate it along with some meat that must have been gums. "Roughage in the diet," I thought. Then he hacked open a fresh skull, scraped aside the half chewed mouthful of lichen which smelled like freshly deposited horse manure, and continued his repast. I had a pilot biscuit.

On my last sally out of the tent before sleeping, I watched fog coming out to meet Elijah and Toby on their way to the longliner.

23 September

This morning a large wet Canadian flag materialized from somewhere and someone found a four-foot plank and "planted the Maple Leaf in the Canadian Arctic." Most of the time it drags limply, though brightly, along the rocks.

Not so bright any more is my moss-green parka cover. When I fold it I notice some areas are now olive green. In spots the rick-rack has worn through and the colour worn off. The zipper on the duffel garment works — with coaxing — past the spot where it has parted company with the coat, while the lining flaps alarmingly. The cuffs are trimmed in the last scraps of the red fox I tanned, now so worn and matted that it resembles dirty cotton batting. The ak£a (brown bear fur) from Aklavik seems to survive all kinds of treatment and, though touched with white from the last time I painted my house, it still spreads long hair across my face, protecting me in winds and blizzards and tickling my nose when I try to catnap.

The canoe full of hunters vanished into a billow of fog leaving the two boats to ride at anchor and me to roam the countryside, occasionally scanning the horizon in the direction the men had taken. I had slept with my damp duffel socks, mittens, and insoles tucked into my sleeping bag. When the things had not dried by morning, I waddled around with the assortment of soggy garments stuffed into my waistband from whence they wandered up and down. I forgot about them until I went to relieve myself and a duffel mitt flopped out. It was only when I went to change the felt insole in my kamiks that I realized I had lost one. I spent a long hour on the tundra searching for it. I have brought only kamiks with me, which are fine on frozen ground but not always a blessing in other situations. Once the canoe was too far from shore for me jump across the water. Toby realized I was stuck, tucked me into the crook of his arm as if he were carrying his little Larry, grabbed a duffel bag in the other hand, and waded ashore with his load.

In the afternoon Elijah and Simagak came for the naphtha and took me with them across the bay to where they had found many caribou. Pita was nowhere in sight. After tea on the beach, Simagak and Toby took Elijah with them and I trudged off behind Natika and Atani across the cold, crunchy tundra. The orange willow leaves were splashes of brilliance among the muted tones of boulders, white

129

patches of frozen lakes, clumps of silvery lichen, and brownish-green moss. We passed two carcasses my partners had evidently killed that morning, then came upon three grazing animals which soon fell under the men's shots. The hunters set about skinning the caribou, leaving me to discover for myself how best to help.

Observing a hunter at the height of his physical powers brings that special pleasure of watching a master at work, no matter what his craft or art may be. The competent hunter goes about the chore of butchering in a business-like manner, slitting the belly, punching the skin away from the underlying muscle, then making further incisions to separate the skin from the fat along the backbone. A tear may run out from the animal's eye as he slashes one side of the face, a tear from the other eye, a bit of toil, and a few hard tugs wrench the skin free. Next he slits the legs lengthwise, etches a circlet around each ankle and strains at the reluctant fur as the other legs of the round-bellied beast flail the air. One more slit around the tail and the heavy brown and white pelt is ready to lay out to dry.

The accomplished hunter's knife slashes with the speed of a darting fish. Just as the face fur is peeled in one seemingly effortless sweep, the legs are also stripped with fluid ease. Sometimes he will not bother to incise around the anus but will twitch the skin off with one sharp tug. The master hunters, jauntily erect, will carry loads as if they were nothing, while others, by their manner if not their words, draw attention to the heaviness of their loads.

My musings were interrupted by Atani, who tossed a caribou skin at me then laughed heartily as I staggered under the bulky fur which had seemed so light as he effortlessly heaved it. When the pelt of the next caribou was free, I picked it up at the rear of the animal. Natika and Atani waited as I walked away with the skin, only to be pulled up short. It was still attached. So I pulled. Then I tugged. The men stood motionless while I jerked and strained until Atani made one small slash around the anus. One more jerk, the skin slipped over the animal's rump and I fell on mine under the mass of flying fur.

Natika removed the bile sac and helped himself to some liver while Atani pushed aside the intestines and carefully slit the bulging stomach. Then he too sliced himself a piece of liver which he dipped into the mushy green contents of the stomach. He took a bite, rolled his eyes, groaned appreciatively, and handed his knife to me. I started with kidney and some of the pure white strings of fat clinging to it, then I tried a tiny dip of green mash on a minuscule corner of liver.

Not bad. Atani scooped out huge handfuls which he ate with relish, but I stuck to tiny amounts eaten with liver. Though it barely touched me, the green smell would not come off my hands for the rest of the day.

By evening the fog had dissipated, my body heat had dried yesterday's apparel and today's felt liners and sheepskin pads in my kamiks were the only candidates for my sleeping bag. Simagak and Toby moved the boats to the next cove; the wind that blew away the fog had also piled up new ice so deep and hard along the shore that the skiff could not get through.

After a leisurely meal of caribou legs and boiled meat, Simagak's buttered, fried pilot biscuits did not provoke much enthusiasm, however, he was again the life of the party when he played back his surreptitious recording of one of the story-telling sessions. Atani twisted and stretched his features into expression of disbelief and appreciation as funny as the fluctuation of his furry, bass voice emanating from the little machine.

24 September

The last day of the hunt was spent packing meat and skins to the shore. The weather was ideally frosty, making the ground firm underfoot. I carried legs and skins, working with Natika and Atani as usual, stopping now and then for a snack from the meat we were packing. Like any day with Inuit, though tiring, it was not without humour. Atani was intrigued with the back-pack Natika had brought but used little. Obligingly, Natika loaded an adult caribou — hind-quarters neatly tucked into thorax — and a whole young animal on the contraption, and Atani set off towards the beach. Halfway there he lost his balance, toppled over, and, like a beetle on its back, lay curled in the snow, kicking and heaving with laughter until Natika came and set him on his feet. After a few trips, I lay down in a pile of skins and dozed off only to be awakened by Elijah's screams of *"Tuqulirama! Tuqulirama!"* ("I'm dying! I'm dying!") Toby was sitting on him, tickling him, laughing and adding a falsetto *"Tuqulirama!"* to the boy's frantic wails. When we climbed into the canoe for the final run back to the boats Atani hoisted me across his shoulder announcing "One more carcass," waded into the water, and dumped me into the craft.

That evening, as the others smoked and spun yarns, I was so tired

131

I couldn't keep my eyes open, let alone follow the conversation. Finally I fell asleep stretched behind the men, parallel with the back wall of the tent. The activity of the men preparing for sleep roused me later, and, much to their amusement, I bounced over to my proper sleeping place, parallel to the right-side wall, like a blue caterpillar on a binge.

25 September

Toby, as the skipper, exudes the aura of the well-born who wear the mantle with a natural dignity and simplicity. His every endeavour — eating muzzles, skinning caribou, cracking bones — seems to be done efficiently and effortlessly. His position in the tent was central, his authority undisputed, and he was regarded with obvious affection by the others. He had worked on the battery charger until after midnight while the other men told stories in the tent. It was he who woke us at 6:30 calling to Atani to light the stove. By 8:30 we were under way.

It was windy but there was no ice to battle on the return trip. Natika cleaned house in the longliner cabin, swept ice off the deck when it was not awash with spray, and manned the galley. He lurched across the wet deck to Toby, at the wheel, with rings of boiled caribou neck, artfully arranged in perfect symmetry on a metal plate. Pita sat on the rolling deck making sandwiches of fat sliced off a seal skin and bits of cold, boiled caribou fished out of the stew pot stowed near the cabin hatch. When the men had been repairing the motor they had rubbed their grimy hands on this fat, then together producing a soap-like lather. Pita will no doubt notice if his crankcase oil needs changing at the next meal. In the cabin, I learned that when the tea is weak, instant coffee is added to produce a palatable brew.

At 8:00 P.M. we passed the last landfall before Igloolik. Toby spread out the nautical chart, pointed out our position and estimated we were about five hours from port. He seemed very tired but decided to push on home rather than camp on the islands. Hardly an hour later we hit very heavy seas which banged the canoe we were towing against the stern. The whaleboat came alongside, but before the combined efforts of all the men could steady the canoe, it again smashed into us, this time stoving in its bow. The men removed the engine, took out the paddles, floorboards, fuel cans, and gear and tried to haul the skittering skiff onto the deck of the mother ship. Finally Natika took a bucket, lowered himself into the bucking craft, and bailed it out, enabling the men to haul it aboard and lash it across the deck.

26 September

At 4:00 A.M., when we arrived opposite the beach at Igloolik and put the canoe in the water to carry us ashore, we had to huddle together in the stern to prevent the split bow from shipping enough water to sink us. The men were staggering from fatigue. Atani rolled his eyes, slid down the side of the beached canoe, announced he would spend the night right there on the ground, and let his head slump onto his chest. In an instant he bounded to his feet, flashed a grin, and hurried off towards home faster than the rest of us could manage.

October

In October, when the bay begins to freeze and there is snow on the land, the snarl of snowmachines once again echoes through the village. In front of his house, Inaq's qamutik lies half buried by last night's storm. The blocks of ice still lashed to it form a miniature alpine landscape glistening in the morning sun. Huge pieces of ice, never quite melting away, circulate year after year in Foxe Basin, gradually becoming a favoured source of drinking water as the sea salt leaches out. Most years some of these blocks lie stranded on the beach in front of the settlement at high tide, forming a playground for children and a ready source of delicious water. However, this week the beach is clear, so yesterday, when a fresh northwest wind sprang up, the hunter towed his long, supple sled across the island to the far shore, where ice was sure to be driven. Unless there is a strong southeast wind to fill Turton Bay with the delicacy before the new ice sets, this is but the first of many trips Inaq and others will make to bring in tea water during the winter.

Last year, before the new water truck could arrive from Montreal by sealift, the old vehicle lay down in a pile of rust and expired before the spring sunlight had returned. The Co-op — unlucky holder of the water delivery contract that year — hired men with motor toboggans and qamutiks to cut lake ice with a power saw then ferry it back to the settlement. When not served by friends, relatives, or neighbours, widows, pensioners, and families whose providers were absent for one reason or another had ice delivered to their houses. For everyone else, the frozen water supply was piled in two central points where people helped themselves. As funds dwindled and workmen were lured onto the trail by the lengthening days, the Co-op appealed to its customers to pick up their ice at the water lake. There the huge, symmetrical excavation sparkled like a brilliant sapphire set in the platinum snow beneath cloud-softened skies, with the gentle hills of Melville Peninsula lying like crumpled velvet in the background.

In May and June, returning seal hunters sometimes stop at Qikiqtaarjuk or Igloolik Point to load ice onto the qamutik next to the fruits of their hunt. More often, however, they make a special trip, taking along a pack of children much as a father in the south will fill the car with his and the neighbour's offspring for a short run to the supermarket to fetch a carton of milk.

3 October

From late summer, when Turton Bay is navigable, until freeze-up, many days may pass when the old women and children have no beached ice to fill their buckets and pans. Yesterday — one such day — children tumbled out of Angut's blue and green canoe and ran up the gravel slope intent on business that only unfettered children understand. Three of the older boys and girls helped pull the canoe onto the shore as Arnak, smiling broadly, approached. The woman held out a large basin into which one of her sons tried to fit an oversized chunk of ice. Laughing and teasing the children, the adults expertly chopped the ice into several containers, then climbed the hill behind the procession of young people, each heading for his or her own house with the treasure. Perhaps some of the lads are working for their Boy Scout Water Provider badge.

4 October

This fall we are profiting from an arrangement the current school principal has made with the University of Alberta to do a credit course in cross-cultural education. It's a great opportunity for me to sit myself down and read all the classics on the North and on education that I never get around to. The forte of the instructor is chairing discussions. Half the students are native and half white, all interested, most interesting, and most have been in the North long enough to have ideas and questions. The perceptions of the Inuit who have been educated in the white man's schools are pertinent and pointed. Sometimes, while helping the non-Inuit to understand the problems caused by the education system under which they studied, the Inuit end up venting their frustration or resentment. Most of the group is open and supportive, while the exceptions among both races force us to clarify our ideas and reasoning. I particularly enjoy the intellectual stimulation. I've always felt that one of the enriching façets of living in a small northern settlement is socializing with types of people you would never meet in the South. People whose interests are so different their paths would never cross in a southern metropolis find it is impossible to remain isolated here since contacts are demanded in day-to-day existence. In such societies, when opinions and ideas have been explored, gossip and drink easily dominate unless people share hobbies or activities like the U. of A. course. In the days before government, when the four white men in a settlement were the Anglican minister, the Catholic priest, the Mountie, and the Bay man, bridge was the common denominator and social salvation of the anglophone societies.

5 October

Levi returned from working another shift at Alert and bought a Polaris snowmachine. Last week Toby, Levi's father, bought a canoe with his cheque for the commercial fishery project he worked on last spring, and the Co-op delivered it this morning. When I saw Sila this afternoon she grinned "Ooo-ah! My son got a new Polaris, my husband got a new canoe, and Housing Association has just given me a new house. All in one day!" Suzie is now living with her boy friend, Natika has gone back to work at Nanisivik, and Tutu and Tommy stayed in Arctic Bay, so the new house will seem large for the couple and the remaining six children.

A new Nursing Station is being built to replace the three trailers now in use. The first of this model was built in Pangnirtung, this second one will incorporate refinements of the Pang station, and the last one will be built at Pond Inlet. When the contract was awarded last spring, a company man came in to assess the manpower, facilities, equipment, and amenities available in the community and arranged to lease one of the two buildings Mark uses as the Transient Centre. The workmen flew in as the ships arrived and were here to receive the construction material and their supplies. They brought a heavy-duty freezer, washing machine and dryer, institutional size pots and pans, kitchen utensils, and cases of foodstuffs to feed their men during the months of construction. Between the Transient Centre buildings they erected a storage "tent" better built than the house I'm living in. There's a layer of plywood, then insulation, another layer of plywood and over all a snug canvas covering. Outside is a fuel tank hooked up to the space heater inside. While they were waiting for their foundation material to be unloaded (foundation material always seems to come off last!) the men installed an exhaust fan in the kitchen, built a storage rack for condiments and cooking utensils, a dining table, kitchen stool, shelves in the storage tent and main building, and generally overhauled their quarters to suit their tastes and convenience. Their cook is a big, hearty man who enjoys company, and, convinced that the chef is the most important person in a northern construction crew, prides himself on his cuisine.

In the other building where I am cooking, there is a bunch of complainers, a bit sharp in their teasing. They irritate me and I find I have adopted the Inuit attitude towards salaried work which annoyed and frustrated me when I first became aware of it. I had been in Repulse Bay less than six months when I wanted another record box made. One of the fathers suggested that a certain young man, whose wife was expecting their first child, was a capable carpenter, unemployed at the time and could use the money. Yes, he said, he would copy my box. A few days passed with no activity so I found some lumber for my friend. The days dragged on, and to each of my queries the artisan would answer that he had not yet finished the box. Thinking it would urge him on, since he declared it to be "almost finished," I paid him for the article. Still no delivery. The priest chuckled at my rantings, pulled on his pipe, and laconically remarked, "He's doing you a favour making that box."

"But I'm paying him for it and he needs the money," I protested indignantly.

"Ha," chortled the priest. "That's the way you see it, but to the Inuk he is doing you a favour."

And now I find I want to snarl at the men in the Transient Centre: "Watch it boys! Tease me too roughly and I'll walk out. I don't *have* to work here and get paid. I'm doing you a favour by cooking for you!"

6 October

The nurses worry about me. Before I started working at the Transient Centre, they wanted to hire me to clean the Nursing Station but government policy forbade their hiring anyone but Inuit. During the early summer they were desperate; there was not a single Inuk in the village who could be persuaded to clean house for them. Now the eye team has just arrived, and, as arranged, I will cook for them during their four-day stay. I cannot be paid money, but there are extra beef steaks, hamburger, eggs, and vegetables among the groceries the doctors brought with them. They are delighted, commending our head nurse saying their work will be easier at Igloolik than anywhere else thanks to her excellent organization. They say they must cook for themselves in other settlements, which is not really a hardship since they bring their own food, but they have more time to work here and welcome the change. It is nice for all of us.

8 October

When I heard a snowmachine stop in front of my house, I looked through the window to see an Inuk standing behind his machine, contemplating a young white husky lying at the end of a rope attached to the rear of the vehicle. Next to the inert mass of fur stood a large white pup with brown ears, looking for all the world like a stubborn burro. In stony unconcern he stood unbudging, not even flicking an eyelash, as the man pulled on the rope to make the other dog stand. The Inuk bent stiff-kneed to peer into the prone animal's face — making sure it was alive, I suppose — and again tugged at the rope, producing a most comical effect. The animal appeared positively catatonic while the man readjusted the stiff front legs in the harness, each leg dropping woodenly back to the ground. Meanwhile Brown Ears stood, not a whisker quivering, as if cast in bronze. Finally the man drove off very slowly with the dogs bracing themselves against the tow ropes but runing in spite of themselves. The resulting humped-up gait had nothing in common with the elegant pulling stance of sled dogs at work.

Light, fluffy snow, glistening like a Christmas card, has powdered the bay white. I'm glad I stepped out last night to see the path of the moon on the dark ice for the last time this year. I took my favourite route home from church, walking along the beach. I was following dog tracks in the fresh snow when I realized — from its sponginess underfoot — that I was on the new sea ice. The dogs were on a spree digging out morsels of fresh seal, leaving bloody tracks on the new snow as they dragged off their booty.

9 October

The first motor tobaggan tracks have appeared on the bay. I hear Tunit got a bear out at camp and Atani brought in the first one for the village. The Hunters' and Trappers' Association has allotted four tags for the camp at Agu Bay, three for Tunit's camp at Ikpikitturjuaq and the remaining eleven for village hunters.

I am out of meat and since it is the rut, caribou is hard to find. This evening I watched men unload seals onto the beach and when I saw two carcasses split open, asked into the deepening darkness if I could have some liver. "Yes," came the immediate reply. I waited, watching, ready to cut out a piece or take home what was given to me. The same voice offered, "I'll bring it over in a little while," so I went home hoping I would recognize whoever it was, for I hadn't been able to distinguish who had spoken. I got out some money and prepared a box of cupcakes in case my benefactor did not wish payment. It was Ikpunu looking for another kind of payment. He's lonesome. His wife is away. He has just returned from working at the mine for several weeks. There are no women there. Some visitors came, joined us for tea and left, and still my lonesome friend stayed on. After he had gone I realized that, in the verbal struggle to persuade him to leave, I'd forgotten to offer him either the money or the baked goods.

Among the Inuit, as among the Japanese that I knew, nudity and body functions are taken as a matter of course. The Inuit view of sex as a natural need — just like eating or sleeping — has amusing implications in my life. Women have offered me their husbands out of kindness, friendship, or even self-interest: the woman may have a "boy friend" but her husband was not being accomodated in like manner.

I find the young men do not always accept a refusal as graciously as do the older men. Once when I returned from the South, a delightful man in his forties was among those who had a big, friendly grin and handshake for me at the airstrip. That evening, to my surprise, he walked into my house and tried to hug me which produced a brief laughing, fumbling scene after which he had tea, chatted, and never returned. A couple of months later, his nineteen-year-old son came to visit, had tea, smoked cigars, conversed hesitantly looking at picture albums, edging ever closer. I found it hard to believe his intentions but had to give up going to the dance that night to give credibility to the polite fibs I used to get him out.

Not so nice was the young man in his twenties who came by one summer night. I could smell no alcohol and wondered if he were high on something else. He was most insistent and when he realized I was not to be persuaded became nasty, saying they were talking about me at their camp. "We don't want you to come camp with us." He even threatened, "You tell people and I'll tell everybody lots of things about you!" No laughing brush-off, "thanks but no thanks" with this lad!

More often advances are made in an atmosphere of horseplay, allowing either option without the ego-damaging refusal. A couple stopped by after I'd finished my carpentry. The topic of discussion was my tender nose and nose-warmer, but the conversation came to an impasse for lack of language skills. The gentleman rose, threw his arms around me, and made as if to rub noses. I was caught completely unawares and they were convulsed at my flabbergasted reaction. She was offering me her husband since my carpentry work, which they had inspected, was done by myself, I explained, "because I have no husband." Obviously, I had missed a link somewhere in the conversation.

Another time, when I was postmistress, an Inuk came by one evening asking for his Family Allowance cheque. He decided he would sleep with me, thereby assuring his place as first in line when the Post Office opened in the morning . . . all proposed with such jocularity that I could not be offended, nor was he demeaned by my refusal.

Yet there is the incident when a lady caught her sixteen-year-old minion in bed with a thirteen-year-old miss and chopped off the hair of the seductress!

12 October

The sight of dog teams and snowmachines on the ice of Turton Bay sent me from house to house looking for someone who would take me out. After many refusals, Inaq agreed to take me along, and we soon joined the others cruising around the ice in the bright sun within sight of the settlement. Each time we met another hunter the men would lament, "There are no seals," then we'd each go our own way looking for aglus and inspecting stretches of open water that looked like rivers, zigzagging around soft ice and water, looking, looking. . . . Inaq made a tight turn and before I knew it I had gently slid off the qamutik onto the ice. I could have grabbed the sled but was afraid I might get hurt being dragged while trying to climb back on board, so I just got up and started walking. As he swung around again, Inaq noticed my walking figure, glanced back to verify that his qamutik was empty, then came and got me. I was embarrassed, for hunters will not take me with them if they have to worry about my doing foolish things like falling off a qamutik. We saw five motor toboggans — a few pulling sleds — and two dog teams during our ritual parade, but no seals.

15 October

Today when I stopped at Simagak's the school children were home for lunch. Fourteen-year-old Elijah and younger Eric look so much alike I at first thought they were twins. Jusipi, nine, was playing with five-year-old Elizabeth and the baby between bites of frozen, raw fish and caribou. Sila and Toby arrived with their three youngest, adding to an uproar like that which was common when they lived there. Even though he works for the Co-op Simagak hunts at night and on the weekends, so the house is surrounded by qamutiks, hunting gear, barrels on which are chunks of meat, and sealskin-stretching frames just as it was when Toby, Natika, and Tommy lived there.

17 October

My nurse friends continue to take good care of me. Now I've been hired for four days to help the technician from Frobisher Bay X-ray everyone in the settlement. One entire family and a small child across the street from them are active tuberculosis cases and medical authorities are looking for a suspected carrier in Igloolik. My job is to take the exposed film out in the darkroom and load the plate for the next photo.

A chartered aircraft used to tour the Arctic annually bringing the X-ray team from Edmonton's Camsell Hospital. Ten years ago in Repulse Bay, it was quite a social event with everyone visiting while waiting in line at the school. You donned the white hospital gown when your turn came and felt important as they produced your card from their file box.

Twenty-five years ago the Inuit were shipped in wholesale lots on the annual resupply ships to sanatoriums in the south. Over the years air travel has replaced the ships, pills have eliminated the prolonged sanatorium bedrest, and the incidence of the disease has diminished.

142

Camsell remains the centre which monitors TB among the Inuit, but now, instead of flying its doctors, technicians, machines, and records through the North, it sends notices to the nursing stations each time X-rays or sputum specimens are required for specific patients. The disease is less terrible now that patients are not removed from their families and communities.

Since the number of those affected has dropped, only active cases and their families are X-rayed regularly, and the administration of medication is entrusted to the families of those involved instead of being distributed through the school or public health nurse and her helpers.

One of the subjects qallunaat debate among themselves is hygiene and health care responsibility and training. Some teachers feel the school is the proper place for children to learn to brush their teeth and they often keep towels at school, scheduling a time for students to enjoy hot showers not available or neglected at home. Others feel the parents should teach their children hygiene and cleanliness as well as give them prescribed medicines. In some schools the medications are given to students on the nurses' lists, and all children are given a daily vitamin. Within the Department of National Health and Welfare guidelines there is some leeway in the amount and type of health care nurses can or must offer. For a short time, there was a nurse in Igloolik who stunned me by announcing over the radio, in English followed by an Inuktitut translation, that optional immunizations would be given at the school. The nurse explained that the parents are responsible for the health care of their children, that she did not want to encroach upon their domain, and if some of them did not want their children to receive the shots, they had merely to notify the Nursing Station to that effect. I never before heard a northern nurse explain to people that they had the right to refuse or accept treatment or that they should approve treatment for themselves or their children. Other nurses prided themselves on their excellent record in vaccinating or immunizing all children and spoke of "building strong youngsters," and "giving the babies a good start in life," as if the children belonged to them or were statistics, not human beings. I must admit, I never thought much about my rights as a patient until that nurse came along.

21 October

My Inuk friend who is married to a white man challenged me for my insistence with the Inuit that I am a qallunaak and therefore different: not adroit at Inuit pursuits but competent in matters of my own culture. She thinks I too often point out my whiteness. My reason had been to make sure people don't measure me against Inuit standards. My friend's point is that I should seek to be evaluated as me, not as a qallunaak. She's right.

The sky is spectacular in a subdued way this evening. Are the white streaks northern lights or clouds? Neither. The smoke is barely rising from the chimneys before spreading out into a low bank of white hanging over the village. A couple of nights ago the northern lights appeared as a green corolla — the first I've seen since I've lived in Igloolik. There has been auroral activity almost every night lately, reminiscent of my good old days in Fairbanks, Alaska; Churchill, Manitoba; and Repulse Bay. I got spoiled living in the aurora belt.

25 October

Friday was a beautiful day with office workers as well as the professional hunters packing to go out on the land. I trotted back and forth visiting houses, running down leads, chasing people all over the settlement, and then . . . success! Around 5:00 P.M. we were off: Tukilaq, Pita, Simagak, his son Eric, and me on three Skidoos and two qamutiks, across the island towards Melville Peninsula. It was windy, nor could we see when we stopped to build shelter for it was the dark of the moon. The snowbank from which the men wished to cut blocks for an iglu was covered by about two feet of soft snow which we all set about pawing away like dogs. With a few deft strokes, Simagak fashioned a block of snow into a cone, hollowed it out and placed a lighted candle in it. That was our illumination until the walls were high enough to break the wind and allow the men to light a lantern. After dinner of frozen raw liver I fell asleep watching the men play patik, betting ammunition and matches amid much gesturing and laughter. Simagak got us up very early to go fishing. We had no luck at the lake where we were camped so went on to another some distance away where our jigging through a hole cut in the ice yielded lots of trout.

I spent most of the day walking over the ice, still translucent without the snow cover winter will pack over it. Sometimes I lay down to watch fish swimming by and to inspect the sandy, pebbly bottom and the shadow patterns thrown on the rippled lake floor by cracks in the ice. Sometimes I got overheated floundering around in drifts among the low, rocky hills between the lakes. I discovered that body heat dries a wet haunch very nicely, after a quasi-disaster when I toppled over into soft snow while struggling with my clothes after relieving myself. I really could survive without such learning experiences but they are not bad in retrospect and, for pedagogical technique, I must admit the method of imparting the knowledge is remarkable enough to imprint a lasting memory.

During the day several parties of fishermen arrived and left. When evening came, since Simagak and Eric had not returned, Pita, Inaq and I built a new iglu. For the first time, no one checked my caulking work, but just moved in when the structure was finished. Luckily I did a good job for in the morning despite the wind there were no holes. Again the two men spent an enjoyable evening playing cards and amusing me with their showmanship so much that I ached from laughing.

On Sunday the men went fishing and I walked for a long time, finally joining them at our second lake. Angut and Atani were fishing with Inaq and Pita. Since my hosts were going to stay out another day to go caribou hunting, I opted to return with Atani. We detoured to a lake somewhere to check a net Atani's son had set under the ice. There wasn't much I could do to help while my companion chopped the ice around the ends of the net, so I walked to warm up my feet. We pulled the net out together, found no fish, and reset the net. We drank hot, sweet tea from Atani's Thermos and I again took my place on the qamutik. There I struggled to keep my nose covered by my scarf and my glasses free of frost while bouncing around on the flying torture instrument, all the while muttering to myself, "Why am I doing this? When I get warm — if I ever get warm — I'll never go out again," knowing full well I'd seize the first opportunity that presented itself. In short, I repeated my customary meditation while travelling on a motor toboggan-drawn sled.

I kept glancing forward, looking for the red light on the radio beacon, but to no avail. After what seemed like an eternity, I was surprised to see the lights of the settlement laid out in a curve of sparkling jewels against the velvet blackness of heaven and earth. As usual, I had had no idea of where I had been and had thought we would come in from the back of the island instead of across Turton Bay.

When I got to my house around 8:00 P.M. my outside door was open and everything inside was frozen, though the stove was on. There was even a thick crust of ice around the water tank. The children had probably come to play and, finding no one home, had left without closing the door.

31 October

"Hallowe'en. Just dressing up and going from house to house saying 'Gimme'!" I muttered. An announcement at noon over CBII says there will be prizes for costumes at a time when thoughtful — perhaps avant-garde — magazines are advertising non-competitive games. "Another instance of the white man introducing something foreign to Inuit culture," I snort. The story I heard about the frustration of the Keewatin teacher in the late 1960s has passed into the oblivion of history: frustration when the first student quizzed answered wrongly and every other student followed suit, not because they didn't know the correct answer, but because they would not embarrass their classmates. Non-competitive, smiling equality then: now, prizes for the best costume. "Bah! Humbug!"

Then the kids start coming around, obviously enjoying themselves, older ones leading younger ones by the hand, all excited, all proud of their costumes. Good, clean fun. No tricks played when treats are not forthcoming; certainly no poison, razor blades, or drugs. It was evident that parents and older brothers and sisters had had fun gussying up the little ones. So I played with them, complimented them, ooh-ing and ah-ing over their get-ups, and slipped a handful of pseudo-jacks into each bulging bag of candy. I even helped put them back together when a scarf started to slip, a set of whiskers drooped the wrong way, or a skirt became a hazard.

After the children had made their rounds, there was a gathering of exotic spirits at the Community Hall. Stockinged faces streaked with make-up hobnobbed with sealskin masks trimmed in wolf or dog fur. Costumes of borrowed clothing and household linens abounded, with all kinds of fur predominating. Someone prowled around in long johns, stuffed front and back, wearing a head-dress of brightly patterned baby sleepers, the legs stuffed into dangling ears which were waved provocatively at all and sundry. I had made myself a bewitching mask and pointed cap, donned a weird assortment of clothes and had ridden up to the Community Hall on the remains of a kakivak found on the beach at low tide, lashed to the end of a broom. Several men were transformed into red-cheeked, scarlet-lipped, bosomy lasses or women so pregnant they could not see over their condition to don matching socks or boots. The non-Inuit community was also well represented. The power plant operator impersonated a tube of toothpaste, one of the nurses was a charming gypsy, and a civil servant arrived in a jingle jangle of strategically placed kitchen utensils. The store manager donned a nurse's whites while she wore the curls and short skirt of a little girl and carried a huge balloon. During the teen dancing in the darkened room, much to the amusement of the onlookers, I chased the balloon, trying to puncture it with my fish spear, until laughter alerted the "little girl" of her peril.

While the contestants were lined up for costume judging, I played croquet with an empty pop can, shooting it between the feet of a bent figure trailing a white fox tail from a mangy caribou-skin qulittaq.

Members of both cultures enjoyed themselves play-acting, dancing, and inspecting each other's costumes. White people admire the original use of everyday materials or the impersonation of items, characters, and other people. However, the Inuit judges immediately eliminate anyone who is recognizable and the entire crowd is hushed as the winner is unmasked. I find it interesting that even when the judges are young people they seem imbued with the values of their elders, for every year the winner is someone unrecognized, dressed in skin clothing. In the intimacy of life in a camp of three or four iglus, where every piece of clothing was as familiar as every face and gesture, only a masterful actor could remain incognito.

Hallowe'en in Igloolik; for the Inuit, an old twist to a new custom; for me, a new light on an old custom.

November

Some of the whites in Igloolik remind me of Americans I knew in Japan who saw the country through the bar-room window. Since they have been here six months the whites are allowed to vote, but they don't know who the people on the ballot are. I feel like the accomplice in something underhanded just because I tell them where this one works, or who that one is. The six-month residency requirement is really inadequate when applied to elections in the Northwest Territories. A Newfoundlander moving to Alberta may *feel* as if he is in a different country, but a basic similarity of culture and language will allow him to grasp, in as little as six months, the concerns and opinions of those around him. But when a Newfoundlander or an Albertan moves to the eastern Arctic, he has to count on an anglophone minority to translate not only the words, but also the concerns and values of another culture. Can someone who will feel like an old-timer if she stays as long as three or four years in her cocoon existence be justified in legislating for the long-time residents? Is it really fair that transient workers whose only interest in the North is the dollars they earn there (to spend in the South) be legally empowered to influence the present and future lives of the real residents of the North?

8 November

The nurses tell me the X-rays from the TB carrier hunt, dispatched via Nordair Air Freight nearly three weeks ago have not yet arrived in Frobisher Bay.

14 November

There were sno-bow feet on either side of the moon last night. I'm sure there's a scientific name for the phenomenon, but to me they look like the bases of rainbows. However, here there would be snow, not rain, hence my term of sno-bow feet for these patches of the spectrum. Today there were grey clouds on which they played then disappeared as the clouds moved on, reappearing as another bank of clouds drifted into range. And now, after dark, there are spectacular northern lights.

Toby and Simagak killed a walrus yesterday, Saturday, and today, after church, their friends and relatives gather at Toby's house. As they enter, visitors leave their boots in the porch, though they do not remove their parkas. On the floor of the utility room, between the porch and the kitchen, a feast is spread on flattened cardboard cartons. Men and women squat, helping themselves to frozen caribou meat and seal fat with ulus and knives provided by the hosts. From time to time an adult or school child will help a toddler who wields a butcher knife he or she has seized, and mothers will partially chew bites before poking them into the mouths of babies in amautis.

Early arrivals regale themselves on the contents of the walrus stomach, poured into a plastic ice cream container. The digestive juices of the animal resemble vinaigrette dressing in which clams and mussles marinate until soft, though still whole, and delicately piquant.

As the feasters finish the frozen course, they move into the kitchen, serve themselves boiled walrus from the pot on the stove, and gather around the dining table picking additional morsels from heaping, steaming community plates. Most of the diners accompany a bite of meat with a bit of boiled fat. Children who demand only fat or only meat are gratified, though those whining for the potato chips they have espied atop the fridge are made to wait in the usually vain hope that they will forget the qallunaak food in favour of the country feast of their elders.

After washing their well-licked fingers in a pan of soapy water and drying them on the greying towel, some guests dip cups into the meat pot while others serve themselves brewed tea or make coffee to their tastes with water from an urn in the kitchen. When the store-bought cookies are all eaten, pilot biscuits appear. Throughout the afternoon, relatives and other friends drift in and out nibbling, laughing, and chatting, listening to the hunters retelling the chase and kill until the cardboard and pot are empty and it is time to go back to church for Evensong.

15 November

After three weeks, my fingers have quit peeling and my feet are no longer sore and swollen. My fingertips were frostbitten while I photographed the building of the first iglu when I went fishing with Inaq and the others. The two weak toes on my right foot also got it again. All of which I consider well worth the enchantment of being on the land and sleeping in iglus. Incomparable!

There's a fascinating "bear team" at the Transient Centre. One of the men has done research on polar bears in the Scandinavian countries, another has worked in Alaska and the rest are either Canadian federal or territorial government wildlife experts. After last night's open meeting with the community they are discouraged. The Inuit again attacked the imposition of quotas by government, asking that natives be allowed to manage their own renewable resources. The experts again explained that the total population of bears in each area determines how many animals hunters in each locality are allowed to kill. They emphasize that the reason for not allowing polar bears to be killed unless the hunter has a tag issued by the government, is to ensure the preservation of the species. The credibility of their data collection program received a set-back if not a death blow from the old man who asked, "Did you know that a polar bear can turn itself into a block of ice?" The experts shook their heads. "Since you don't even know that," the elder queried, "how can we believe all these things you are telling us about bears?"

The dark is the meeting season for the close to twenty local committees: Hunters' and Trappers' Association, Housing Association, Alcohol and Drug Education Society, the church groups, Local Education Authority, Recreation Committee, Radio Society, Land Claims Office, etc. The committee officials who receive stipends have gotten on to a good thing. Instead of calling meetings at night, they've started announcing their meetings for "three in the afternoon: come and have coffee." During working hours they get paid their salaries and also their stipend for attending the meeting, and are free to go to the movie or another meeting in evening. So much for the unsophisticated, naïve Inuk!

Along with the three o'clock committee meetings, the forthcoming visit of the Commissioner was announced over the radio this afternoon.

18 November

Igloolik, the convention centre of the North! Ten women from Nain, Labrador, leave tomorrow after ten days here; the Co-op Federation Board of Directors and the Inuit Tapirisat Board of Directors have both scheduled meetings here, there is talk of Attagutaluk School hosting the regional school conference this spring, and some thirty game people comprising Hunters' and Trappers' Association delegates from all Baffin settlements and game officers from Baffin, Yellowknife, Winnipeg, and Ottawa start meeting today. There were already three planes from Yellowknife on the strip last night when the local sched arrived. The hunter delegates arrived in time for the farewell dance for the delightful Nain ladies who have stolen the hearts of everybody here. Discussions with them have been a revelation for the local people. The policies of the government of the Northwest Territories for natives are unheard of in Newfoundland – Labrador. Our ladies were stunned to hear that Nain women sometimes could not get welfare because they could find no interpreter to present their case for them. In our settlements it is taken for granted that the government will provide interpreters at any time, any place, not only free to the user, but at an elegant salary for the interpreter. Northern Low Rental Housing was much admired by the visitors who must provide whatever housing they can at their own expense. They were incredulous when they learned that fuel and electricity are included in the modest, subsidized rents. "My electricity bill alone is $75" gasped one Nain lady upon learning the minimum rents had been raised from $3 to $5.*

Two women are happily sewing caribou clothing for some of the delegates to the Hunter's and Trapper's Associations meeting.

The Commissioner's visit was interesting, as usual. The southern newspaper men and women in his entourage exclaimed, as usual, "Everybody smokes!" and, as usual, were appalled at the sight of young

*The minimum rent in 1981 was raised to $30, which includes fuel, electricity, water delivery, and sewage and garbage disposal.

children puffing on cigarettes. Amid the usual ambience of children making various play noises, with the usual smell of smoke and diapers getting heavier, and the library getting stuffier, the general meeting wore on. Mark Evaluardjuk, in deference to his position as a Member of the Legislative Assembly, was at the head table. When the discussion turned to proposed Education Ordinance he spoke, disassociating himself from his government colleagues along the table. Consummate politician that he is, Commissioner Stuart Hodgson made some gracious remark flattering Mark, and then the assembly bared its teeth and sprang to the attack.

Simagak was forceful and amusing (making a nice subject for a Toronto newspaper photographer). Fr. Lechat asked for a policy statement explaining the government's aims of education, a theme picked up by several Inuit. Atani asked how long the government had been working on this ordinance. The Commissioner went on for a second time at great length detailing the steps taken since 1969. To which Atani replied, "You whites have been working all these years without a word to the Inuit, and now you're asking us to study your proposal and decide in one month whether we want it or not!"

Inaq put on a good show talking about what children should be taught: navigation on the barrens using the ripples on the snow, stars, wind, etc. He knelt on the floor between the Commissioner's party and the crowd, drew on the carpet, and used his whole body as well as gestures, facial expressions, and voice inflection to put his ideas across. His presentation was punctuated by grunts and groans of assent from the spectators. Old Siaku, dressed in white shirt and tie, voluminous pants pleated around his waist by a leather belt whose tail hung to his knees — made his customary speech thanking the Commissioner for coming, praising him and the white men for the great things they have brought the Inuit, and telling the guests how much the white man has improved the lot of the Inuit.

Then there was a unanimous vote asking for a year to study the proposed Education Ordinance.

21 November

The evening tanning classes which Sila has been attending in the school technical centre are over after weeks of retting, rinsing, stretching, and scraping. Her reaction is a shrug and the comment, "My skins are that soft without so much time doing all those things." I wonder if the tanned skins will wear any longer than the traditionally prepared ones but will probably never know since it would mean asking questions to determine the comparative life of articles made with processed or untanned skins. That's the type of project anthropologists can do but which I cannot. The Inuit expect each new crop of visitors to ask the same questions, and they know that the profession of anthropologist demands the prying open of forgotten memories, indiscreet questions, and probings into the innermost thoughts of the subjects. There are several old people in the village who make a good living as professional "informants," and one shrewd anthropologist laughed with me about the perfect staging and delivery provided by a lady who just happened to be recommended to him by her bilingual granddaughter . . . as if the prospect of speaking with a white man about the old days was a new and exciting idea.

Envy taints my view of anthropologists, scientists, museum curators, students, government workers, visitors, tourists, and all the other people who learn more about the settlement in their short stays than I will in years. But I have years in which to learn. The subjects of their queries are my friends and neighbours and I cannot make a nuisance of myself by prying into their affairs. Inuit are wont to complain that qallunaat are always washing and always asking questions. I continue to wash, but I have learned to wait and see or remain uninformed, and when I do inadvisedly pose an unnecessary question, the answer is laughter or mockery.

I have also been alienated by "researchers" who arrive with a conclusion which they set about proving — a trick as old as the title "anthropologist" but nonetheless annoying. Sometimes questions that I think would be fit dissertation themes pop into my mind, like that tanned skin question, or how much dilution of Inuit blood there must be before babies are no longer born with the oriental spot. I can just imagine the reaction if I were to go from house to house inspecting the bums of babies of interesting parentage! Yet university students have conducted research demanding a comparable invasion of privacy with the co-operation of the Inuit, and I enjoy measuring their findings against my own experience and observation. Now and again I am surprised to discover a trait or habit noted by early explorers has not disappeared with the snows of yesteryear as I had supposed, but still exists.

This afternoon at Angut's, where I visit fairly often, when I picked up a cup to serve myself, my hostess grabbed it from me and rushed to the cupboard, proclaiming, "You can't use that. You're a qallunaaq," and got me a clean cup. In order not to feel deliberately insulted, I have decided she was trying to show her out-of-town guests that she knows how to entertain white people. My compensation came when I stopped by Inaq's and squatted to help myself to some raw frozen fish from the cardboard in front of the stove. As I started to cut myself a portion, Alitsiaq, kneeling beside me, scornfully chided *"Tamma-ravit,"* ("You're doing it wrong,") and patiently showed me how to start from the skin side and cut to the bone, then parallel to the bones, producing a fillet.

I spilled some tea by my bed last night, and wiped it up without putting on the light. This morning I picked up the frozen tea I had missed and threw it into the sink to melt.

30 November

Toby and Sila's son Levi and Laura were married along with three other couples in the Anglican church this evening. The brides all wore long white gowns and veils — some of them familiar to those who have attended previous Anglican weddings here. Each bride came down the aisle on the arm of her father or a surrogate, one dressed in a suit, the others in jackets of varying hues, patterns, and fits, but nonetheless indicating the solemnity of the occasion. The grooms were likewise formally attired in shirts and jackets, two with ties, and all had temporarily put aside their blue jeans in favour of trousers.

When the couples were duly paired off, lined up with their backs to the congregation and "fathers" were in place, the pastor — Canon Noah Nasook resplendent in black cassock and graceful, billowing white surplice, Order of Canada rosette neatly stuck on his wide stole — worked his way back and forth along the row asking "Who gives this woman?" and "Do you take this man. . . ?" distributing rings and imparting blessings. During the final hymn, those who wished to photograph the newlyweds were invited into the sanctuary where the scene was continuously illuminated by flashes from cameras as the couples buried their noses in their hymnals. The last note signaled the end of the churching ceremony and the beginning of the lay festivities. The brides were seated in the sanctuary facing the congregation and Canon Nasook took his place, beaming among the grooms standing behind their ladies. When the camera clicks abated, the pastor posed, the flowing sleeves of his ample surplice protective wings around the shoulders of each couple, as he paternally enfolded them in a photogenic gesture. Next the parents were called to stand with their wedding pair, family by family, and finally the entire group faced the photographers.

Then came the presentation of gifts. The donors were arrayed in holiday finery and the children and other close relatives of the brides were the first to come forward. Reverend Nasook, the gracious host, provided a running commentary, identifying those tendering gifts and adding comments and drolleries which were greeted with laughter and applause. Piles of brightly wrapped parcels smothered the brides and spilled onto the floor around them before people finally began to leave the church.

In the middle of the road sat the water tank truck. When the street was full of people, Marcusi, the water-truck driver turned on the headlights and his accomplice climbed onto the rocks around a power pole to throw handfuls of goodies through the light beams into the darkness where well-wishers scrambled in the snow collecting sticks of chewing gum, miniature candy bars, and hard candies. Last to leave the church were the minister and the bridal parties who wove through the festive crowd towards the rectory on the hill behind the church. After signing the marriage papers and enjoying tea and sweets with Nasook and his wife, the couples repaired to the home in which they are living — some with the groom's parents, others with the bride's — to open gifts among friends. A steady stream of Inuit went from house to house until late in the evening, feasting with the newlyweds and their families. Children flitted through the darkness, appearing in a doorway, watching silently, then darting out to chatter among themselves on the way to another house. There they again waited quietly at the entrance, their eyes begging to be invited in, tumbling off towards yet another reveller's home when an invitation was not forthcoming.

For decades Christian missionaries have tried to inculcate into their devotees God's marital commandment of one per customer . . . with no more success here than elsewhere in the world. There is not the effort to conceal the less than perfect observation of this precept among Inuit as there was in more densely populated areas of Christendom. Trial marriages were practical arrangements, accepted by some missionaries, in the days when all unions were arranged by the elders. As fate would have it, just when the missionaries seemed to be

instilling at least a consciousness of the Christian dictate as conflicting with local preference and practice, trial marriages, cohabitation
without marriage, and single parenthood burgeoned as acceptable in
other societies.

Nobody here has ever been surprised that those churched in white
have lived together, usually for several years, and have at least one
baby. Ideas of romantic love are sweeping in through magazines,
radio, and personal contact with whites visiting the North or from
Inuit sojourning in the South, but the persistent attitude of many
older couples fascinates me. The good of the individual was subordi-
nate to the good of the traditional community in which the family was
the stable, basic unit of society. Family love existed, and exists today,
independent of physical attraction. I grew up with the idea that sex is
the ultimate expression of commitment, fulfillment of the affection
and love which causes persons to share their lives. Here I know loving
couples, the nuclei of large, loving families, one or both of whom
have a lover on the side. Such arrangements are general knowledge,
and, even in cases where a partner does not like sharing the sexual
favours of his or her spouse, the home is not threatened by what my
standards label continued infidelity.

Ideas of feminine comeliness are also evolving — or eroding. The
early explorers remarked on the beauty of the Inuit clothing produced
by the artistic working of skins into pleasing patterns, the use of
ermine tails and beads, and wrote of women braiding their hair onto
boards. A lass in Repulse Bay used to jingle pleasantly as she walked by
in her amauti whose fringe swayed musically under the weight of
glittering empty .22 cartridges. She still carries her latest baby in her
amauti but has exchanged her kamiks for high-heeled boots, wears a
nursing bra, curls her hair, and paints her eyes and mouth.

December

1 December

Anna has moved into the tent-shed she built last summer. It now lies under a white dome amid a litter of seal skins on stretching frames, snowmachine parts, and snow-encrusted caribou skins hanging above a half-buried qamutik and a wooden box. Scattered bits of paraphernalia and clothing will be buried by the next spate of blowing snow, after which another layer of toys, clothing, rags, and bric-a-brac will be strewn over the whiteness like seeds until it too is ploughed under by the northwest winds.

I bent low to enter and squatted by the wooden door on the beaten snow floor, next to the carving area, until my glasses readjusted from bright sun to yellow lantern light. Anna was enthroned on caribou skins spread across the back of the room, comfortable in her flowered dress, legs outsretched, her lap covered by the skin she was sewing. She welcomed me with a smile, put aside the skin, threaded a needle with sinew, and sewed a plastic button on a small sweater. Behind her, pre-school Rosa and a neighbour's child played on the sleeping skins, rolling into the trunks lined against the canvas wall.

In the eight-by-ten-foot structure were mounds of clothing, skins of various animals, clutter and niceties including all the fixings to serve visitors tea and biscuits, frozen meat or fish, and a qulliq over which hung the teakettle. The carving corner, covered with dust, was littered with hammer, drill, file, hacksaw, and axe, and a chipped butcher knife. A couple of lumps of green stone beginning to take the shape of seals lay among the pieces of antler, whale teeth, walrus teeth, and bones. Light came from stone and naphtha lamps rather than through the plastic window sagging darkly under the snow pressed against it. Anna laughed heartily when I explained that my swollen lip was from biting it while trying to chew my kamiks into a better fit. While I drank tea and ate caribou quarq, she sewed rosettes of thin ujjuk skin strips onto the soles of the offending footwear to keep me from slipping and sliding so much.

5 December

A new white family has arrived and the woman is nice enough but different. She asks questions: "Where are you going?" "What are you going to do this afternoon?" Possibly the main reason there is a semblance of harmony, and certainly no open hostility, in the non-native community is that each person respects the privacy of all the others. None of us would phone to ask, "What are you doing?" but rather, "Are you busy?" More than a matter of semantics, it is the verbal expression of a way of thinking. Notwithstanding strong conflicting opinions among us women, we all get along well. The new arrival has not yet learned to let a subject drop when it is obvious that agreement is not forthcoming. She seems to regard people with differing opinions as opponents to be convinced, which upsets the gay tranquility nurtured by the rest of the whites, who are kind, hoping she will eventually calm down. I fear she may be influenced by the talk of the Co-op mechanic who is quitting . . . again.

The Co-op provides his house, a food allowance, and a salary. His wife was glad to come to a settlement far from the closest liquor store but fate conspired against her, for he found a kindred spirit here with whom he could drink and damn his surroundings. It is easy to understand why he is unhappy. He told me that he had quit school after the sixth grade, at thirteen years of age, to become an apprentice mechanic at a very low wage, and he complained bitterly about the local apprentices.

The Igloolik Co-op had obtained funds to train mechanics in its shops, but our friend claims that when the students arrived — late — in the morning, they only played. In exasperation he called a halt to the training experiment. He is irritated, not to say infuriated, by the Inuit, who, according to him, have everything handed to them without any apparent effort on their part. The seeming lack of relationship between work performed and wages received galls him, and he could not accept, ignore, or even tolerate the unreliability of Inuit as regards working hours. Obviously the memory of struggling out of bed and sleepily dragging himself through the cold and dark to work when other boys his age were enjoying school, haunted him and made him bitter and resentful towards a people who seem free of pressure from timetables. He preferred to forget that they may spend twelve or fourteen hours at the floe edge and remembered only that they sleep until noon. He did not grasp their feeling of responsibility for providing for their families through hunting but only saw them cheerfully setting off for game at any hour.

The other thing that rankled is the Inuit lack of concern for material things. The wage economy, as introduced into Inuit land by the government and some co-operatives and missionaries, has few points in common with the Protestant ethic and WASP-country economic philosophy lived by the mechanic and most other North Americans. Like the prizes in Cracker Jack boxes, money is shovelled out with seemingly no correlation between effort and recompense. Indeed, the material trappings of mercantile society are considered to be something due the Inuit rather than the fruits of toil. In traditional pursuits Inuit produce what they need. For example, a harpoon may represent for the hunter the discomfort and effort in procuring the materials, plus the hours of work necessary to fashion it, in addition to the nebulous value of the expertise that comes from years of experience and practise in the making of such an item. This structuring of value is not present in the material things that have been recently introduced into the North. Labour for wages has not been linked with value of objects, nor have imported items been allotted recognized worth by the Inuit. Hence the carelessness which so annoyed the mechanic who witnessed the insouciant destruction of material things by adults as well as children.

6 December

Hobbies have been the salvation of many in the North: badminton, brewing, volleyball, floor hockey, bridge, cross-country skiing, and among the group here this year, indoor gardening and gourmet cooking. Fortunately, I'm content to exist indefinitely on caribou, canned tomatoes, and frozen spinach, for I have never enjoyed an income in the north that would permit me to cosset myself with imported gastronomic delicacies. When I first came to the Northwest Territories nothern gourmet cooking meant the challenge of making government rations not only edible but interesting. There followed years when mail and produce vied for the honour of most welcome freight on plane days. Today, satellite telephone and jet aircraft make possible a type of cuisine more readily recognized as universal gourmet. When conversations turn to speculation or tales of woe about the arrival of food orders, produce in the stores, or the merits and demerits of suppliers, I commiserate or rejoice as indicated, but as a spectator rather than participant. I have, however, succumbed to the mania for exotic teas and am a slave to my houseplants.

Over the years, through the generosity of friends moving south, I have accumulated potting mixtures, vermiculite, peat, and other soils I don't understand, and I gleefully join in the trading of slips and seedlings. Some government employees arrive from the South each fall with potted plants and others who attend winter meetings are apt to return with a slip or cutting protected from the cold in the breast pocket under their parka. One house boasts a three-foot-high avocado and a philodendron of like proportions growing out of a huge box of imported soil. Another couple, who have gone in for hydroponics, eat lettuce and tomatoes all winter. At the height of the vacation season, the few whites left in the village can be seen making the rounds to water plants in vacationers' homes. My stove has no thermostat and therefore must be readjusted with every change of wind and weather. I have asked friends to baby-sit my house and returned to find them desolate, once because everything had frozen and another time because the house had become so hot the plants all died, and candles, carbon paper, crêpe soles, etc. melted. To find your plants frozen is the more traumatic because they look perfectly all right until the house is warmed up, and they start to thaw. As they turn brown and limp you realize that it was ice, not life, that preserved their greenness and held them erect. To avoid such traumas, if I am to be away any length of time, I put my plants and canned goods out to board with friends in warm houses and let my house freeze up.

Dwarf marigolds are my favourite houseplant and lettuce my most delicious. One of these years I will build myself a greenhouse and raise lettuce and chard. . . or get a larger house and go in for hydroponics. In the meantime one of the missionaries gave me a five-gallon wine jug to use as a terrarium. Though I planted flower seeds, it was a melon vine amid a lush growth of grass that crowded towards the narrow neck of the bottle. The vine waved tendrils tentatively over the edge, then leapt with abandon out of the jar into the summer sun, raced across the window, up the wall, and along the ceiling towards the light fixture before the weakening fall sunlight curbed its ambitious peregrinations.

9 December

Christmas fever is mounting; decorations are for sale at the Bay and the children are preparing the Christmas Concert. Inaq came into the Bay today with a bright crocheted sack, from which I drew my gift name. I wanted a woman's name so traded with the cashier, who preferred a man's name. We both burst out laughing for we had traded husband for wife.

12 December

Natika phoned, saying he had just arrived from Nanisivik and will bring over a parcel from friends in Arctic Bay. More fuel to the Christmas spirit.

14 December

There was an interesting charade during mass. The woman in front of me took a small sleeping baby out of her amauti and thrust it into the arms of the four-year-old boy beside her. She then tried in vain to stuff a kicking, struggling two-year-old into the pouch, eventually acquiescing and sending him across the aisle to his father. But the latter was dozing, so she scooped up the two-year-old, leaned across the man on the aisle, and tapped her husband on the forehead. Still nodding, he took the child onto his lap while Mama collected the baby from the four-year-old and proceeded to nurse it.

During the past few weeks there have been announcements for meetings, rehearsals, benefit sales, decorating corvées, choir practices, gift-wrapping parties, and many other preparations for Christmas. This week CBII has been announcing the starting time of the Cub and Boy Scout Carnival for "Friday night, December 13, after church." Last night local residents were invited to donate to the equipment and uniforms fund by playing various games of chance, guessing the number of bubble gums in the jar or the weight of a grocery hamper, or by buying tickets on a beautiful cake depicting a saluting Scout, complete with ribbon and badges. If you tired of trying to hit the balloon with the money in it, or navigating the electrical maze without ringing the buzzer, you could enjoy the children's gallery of drawings around the gym walls. Amid Baby Jesus portraits and holly wreaths an extraordinary reindeer clings stiffly to the pitched roof of a red brick house while alongside, Santa and sleigh fly dizzily above sky-scrapers and pine trees. An adipose Santa in red regalia, at the handlebars of a John Deere motor toboggan, pack securely lashed to the qamutik behind him, looks as if he will drive through the forest of Christmas trees hung with baubles and gilt letters spelling J*E*S*U*S, right into the large, truly northern landscape painting of gently rolling, treeless hills, all blue and white behind a tiny blue and white village.

The Cub and Boy Scout Carnival netted $580. No one has tried to tally the net enjoyment it provided.

17 December

My house is a veritable fairyland of tinsel icicles illuminated by coloured lights massed in three windows. Suzie and Sally helped hang a profusion of prettily shaped cookies on coloured yarn bows from the electric cable around the walls and across the ceiling and from anywhere else they could find to hang them. Many houses boast outdoor lights and several people have mounted loudspeakers on their roofs. Christmas carols waft through the neighbourhood, unless the occupants have turned on the radio, which may rend the serenity with a jet of rock music and chatter. Every year there are more artificial Christmas trees and mangers. Urqsu has figures surrounding the Christ Child on a bed of plastic hay with a scarlet-coated RCMP standing guard on horseback.

Inuit are now clad in the kamiks whose ujjuk soles women chewed as they walked to the store for their Christmas shopping, and everyone is wearing some new, colourfully embroidered piece of clothing. The final feast food has also arrived: caribou and walrus cached in the summer and now deliciously high, which hunters have recently retrieved from Baffin Island.

The furnace has been lit in the stone church, and, on the arched façade, coloured lights brighten the darkness of day in this land where "day" does not always presuppose light, nor "night" darkness. The Anglican church is also decorated; peering from the sanctuary win-dow is a Santa whose eyes follow shoppers on their happy errands.

Inside he smiles from the lectern as well, and a phalanx of Santas, elves, angels, and pixies presides over the altar while two huge Christmas trees twinkle in the corners of the sanctuary. Garlands and sparkling ornaments encircle the walls and march across the ceiling, some even clinging to the appliquéd tapestry behind the altar. The wall hanging depicting the local scene of Hudson's Bay store, Anglican church, Inuit, dog sled, and various animals has been enlivened by glittering candles and figures, including a rotund snow man who seems to be bounding out of the store onto the back of a large black dog.

18 December

Tonight the Yuletide season was officially initiated by the annual Christmas Concert. In previous years all offices and stores closed and services were suspended while the entire community gathered at the school to be entertained by the students. Alas! The times they are a changin'. Capitulating to consumer society, the people now hold the concert in the evening to enable the stores to stay open and still permit their personnel to see their children perform. It is said that keeping offices open was also a consideration determining the evening performance. Too bad, for I always thought it delightful that government — for that is what the offices pertain to — could wait while the community was governed by the pleasure of celebrating together.

Tussles with the curtain were the leitmotif punctuating the flow of skits, songs, and dancing choruses performed by each class from kindergarten through grade nine. There were the usual unruly beards and pillow stuffings and angels wearing sealskin boots. The stage was awhirl with beggars, soldiers, royalty, seals, mice, cats, bride and groom, and hunters clapping, turning, singing, and shuffling singly and in groups, with a sprinkling of crawling if not prancing caribou-clad reindeer galloping off in all directions. This year's rendition of "The Night Before Christmas" was unique, with English narration, lines spoken in Inuktitut, and hilarious liberties with the plot. The popularity of Laurel and Hardy movies was evidenced by the grade seven pie-in-the-eye fracas which delighted the audience, and the Toothbrush Rock of grade five, if translated into English, would make a fine television commercial. But the grade two's, with their enthusiastic singing dramatization of a seal hunt, and their self-made costumes were the show stoppers.

From the opening grade three story in Inuktitut of the little cripple who offers his crutches with the gifts of the Wise Men at the crib and runs away cured, to the final rousing grade four bilingual chorus of "We Wish You A Merry Christmas," the audience beamed its delight and pride, parents coming forward to take flash photos as their youngsters appeared on stage. The offerings were mainly in Inuktitut with one or two in English and the rest in both languages. However, the rapt attention of the audience, followed by smiles, laughter, and applause, were proof that comprehension was not a prerequisite for enjoyment.

28 December

Everything's awhirl in my brain, as is normal during Christmas and Easter weeks. I not only lose track of what day it is but also of whether it is day or night. It really doesn't matter. There's always something going on: people visiting, dancing, playing games, movies, church services.

The stone church was jammed full as it always is for Midnight Mass and the Easter Vigil Service. In the sanctuary, livid pink and vivid blue plastic flowers, emerald green fronds, and gold syllabics announcing "He Is Born" were pinned to banners behind the altar. A profusion of bright imitation flowers hung with silver tinsel were festooned in spirals around the stone, iglu-shaped tabernacle. Coloured lights, a huge multicoloured metallic star, and tinsel streamers enlivened the manger scene with Mary and Joseph, carved locally, and an imported, bisque, blond Baby Jesus. During the service the Catholics delighted in belting out the Latin Mass many of them learned as students of the Grey Nuns in Chesterfield Inlet. Everyone joined in all the verses of Inuktitut translations of such traditional carols as "Adeste Fideles," "It Came Upon A Midnight Clear," and "Puer Natus." By 2:00 A.M. Santa was distributing gifts in the mission while washtubs of tea were being prepared in the kitchen. Box upon box of pilot biscuits were distributed by handfuls to the revellers, more than one of whom stuffed a few extra into his pocket or her purse. To my great delight, whoever drew my name carved me an ivory and soapstone pendant, but no one will tell me who made it or who gave it to me.

The Anglican gifts were distributed in church after the Christmas morning service. When people had had time to feast after church, they began to drift into the R.C. Mission where games continued all afternoon until 7:00 P.M. Evensong and Benediction. People played for a while, went home to eat or sleep, or visited, then came back to play some more. The great favourite, nugluktaq, kept the crowd engrossed and players roaring their frustration or elation until the targets were tied up close to the ceiling and musical-chairs-dancing held sway. There was no scheduled community activity after the church services, leaving the evening free for family dinners and visiting.

After noon on December 26, the Anglican men piled the church benches neatly in the snow outdoors, and the festivities started off with the Sunday School Pageant. It was very elaborate this year, beginning with songs by a massed choir of children eight years and older. There were marvelous costumes; imposing personages and animals, and flowing beards and moustaches that wobbled, fell off, and were retreived and replaced. A narrator at the microphone read while actors portrayed Abraham's sacrifice, an angel announcing the imminent birth to Joseph, Romans taking a census, and the birth of Jesus and his "lying in a manger."

Games started off with devotional contests offering prizes for the one who could name the most books of the Bible, or who could correctly identify the greatest number of dates as saint's days or holy days, and so on. By the time these games were about to end, there were quite a few white people there so Nasook announced a contest for them: a prize for the one who could write out the "Our Father" the fastest. Play continued with musical-chair-dancing, parlour games, and Inuktitut tests of strength, ending around 6:00 P.M. when the prizes, if not the competitors, were exhausted. Over the radio that night it was announced that Rev. Nasook and Fr. Lechat would officiate at the opening of the season's games and dances at the Community Hall at 9:00 P.M.

When I feel like it I go out prowling to join whatever group is in action at the moment. Last night the action was at the Mission. Someone had brought a drum, and, as the word spread, more and more people arrived. When I got there Atani and Toby were singing ai-yi songs over the microphone while one man after another claimed the drum, dancing in a cleared space surrounded by the crowd. Some rolled the drum in a wide arc, striking the rim in the air with the thick stick. Others bent low, their whole bodies curved over the instrument, then straightened as they raised the skin-covered ring. Some held the drum handle in their right hand and the stick in their left; still others held the drum in the left hand. Old people, young people, teen-agers, and even a couple of ten- and twelve-year-old boys had their turn, each applauded by the circle of spectators. The clothing of the dancers was as varied as their styles. Some wore kamiks, plaid flannel shirts, and crocheted caps, others parkas and heavy boots with felt liners, and one young man was resplendent in a black leather jacket with silver studs. After the dancers had tired and time had been allowed for tea at home, people wandered up to the Community Hall where games organized by various groups continued until the lights were dimmed and the band started blasting forth their music for teen dancing. Studies indicate many Inuit now have hearing loss attributed to their constant use of snowmachines. I suspect their fondness for "the-louder-the-better" type music may be a significant factor.

Some events are announced over the radio around mid-afternoon; no one seems to be up this week to put the station on the air at the scheduled noon hour. There have been no outdoor activities, for it has been cloudy and windy during the couple of hours of midday pink light. People are being urged to form groups and prepare acts for a variety show announced for New Year's Day.

January

2 January

By 11:30 P.M. on New Year's Eve, St. Matthias Anglican church was bursting with women carrying babies in amautis, excited youngsters, restless teen-agers, and men arrayed like a cloud of peacocks. As the last hymn died away, Canon Nasook tugged on the bell rope, wishing everyone a Happy New Year. People streamed from the warm church into the cold darkness, their breath rising in white clouds. Women rocked from one foot to the other as children chased a litter of fat pups amid the tangle of feet. Shots rang out as the men grabbed the rifles they had leaned against the building. Red and yellow flares shot into the air from all over the settlement, punctuated by more and more pops of rifle fire, and children painted silver arcs across the velvet night with sizzling sparklers. On Canada Day we have twenty-four hours of sunlight and no fireworks. On New Year's Day the sun does not rise, and, though the darkness is perfect for fireworks, temperatures hovering around −40°C do not encourage extended displays. Even before the last Roman candle balls of cascading colour evaporated, people were walking home or to friends' houses for hot tea and sweets or boiled caribou and seal before the last dance of the season.

Sila and Toby came by my house with their three youngest and later two more of their children arrived along with one of the teachers and her mother. Sila and Toby have always eaten anything I've offered them: homemade pizza, which can be pretty weird, soups, stews, casseroles. The only thing Sila won't try is the wine and liquor which I offer at New Year. Consequently I served Sila tea while her husband tasted some liquor which he avowed he didn't like. I poured him a glass of wine which he denigrated in turn, so I gave him tea too. We chatted and sipped filling the glasses and cups until my glass ran dry. I turned to take the Kahlua Toby had spurned to find he had finished it and was working on the wine.

The pre-dance games didn't start until after 1:00 A.M. While people were arriving at the Community Hall, a strip dance drew much comment and hoots of laughter from participants and spectators alike. Dancers were retired when the music stopped and the MC commanded, "All people wearing red socks, sit down," or "Anyone wearing long johns, out!" The command to all wearers of false teeth wiped out one generation and a cigarette ban seated another.

A braiding contest found the floor covered with couples sitting facing each other, legs outstretched, soles touching those of the partner, yarn between them, waiting for the "Go." Not only the speed with which the round, four-strand braid was completed, but also the evenness of the work determined the winners. Next, lady dancers were given a swatch of material, needle, and thread and told to patch their partner's trousers when the music stopped. There were yowls as well as cries of frustration mingled with the laughter as seamstresses jabbed frantically with their needles during the short bursts of silence between long stretches of rock music. A comely southern visitor being pressed to join a contest "for those over forty-five" could not countenance the invitation as other than the insult it would have been in her native culture, despite her host's explanation that, in this society that reveres the aged, the invitation was a compliment.

Finally, when the hall was packed, those over sixty — nine men and women — were each claimed by a "parent" with a baby bottle full of soda pop. The parents sat on the floor, took their charges on their laps or into their arms as best they could, and fed them their bottles. One "baby" got so tickled he burst out laughing, spraying his "papa" and nearby spectators. His neighbour repeatedly tried to look around to see how the others were doing, but each time her "mama" grabbed her head and stuffed the bottle farther into her mouth while she squeaked with bugging eyes. The winning pair was beautifully matched. Papa Simagak stroked baby's cheeks and bearded chin and cooed soothingly while baby Siaku gulped the bubbly liquid.

I hear the dance continued until ten in the morning.

When I got up New Year's Day I started the year with walrus and Winzertanz with a chaser of Muenster cheese.

The variety show provided a fitting grand finale for the Christmas season. There were several more or less musical combos, one in outlandish costumes and make-up whose music was as mixed as the music makers, who turned out to be two hunters, the store clerk, and a mother of twelve. The antics of a middle-aged couple imitating the gyrations of the young peoples' dancing, which might have been censored for a southern audience, drew gales of laughter here. There was a juggling exhibition by a giggling line of housewife chorines, several ai-yi singers, drum dancers, and the winners, a pair of housewives who did throat singing. In the evening no admission was charged for the movie *Charlotte's Web*. The lights of the Community Hall were out by midnight for on the morrow — today, that is — school and office hours are supposed to return to normal.

3 January

The Annual General Meeting of the Co-op was scheduled to start at 1:00 P.M. at the R.C. Mission. Reasoning that meetings never start when scheduled, I didn't go until two and found they were already on the second item of the agenda. Across the width of the room Board members, the store manager, and the general manager sat behind tables littered with papers, ash trays, pop cans, and foam cups. Beside them, cases of soft drinks were stacked against the wall, and cups, tea, coffee, milk, sugar, and an urn of hot water were laid out on a table in the corner. Adults sat on church benches while behind them children played King-of-the-Mountain on the back rows. As the meeting wore on, adults and children came and went. Each time the door opened, a blast of white air billowed along the floor and whirled upwards, disturbing the layer of smoke hovering below the ceiling.

The same people had much to say about each item on the agenda and many people spoke at length about co-operating with the Hunters' and Trappers' Association in the construction and use of a freezer, the pros and cons of charging interest on overdue accounts, price and quality of handicraft and sewing items, the purchase, packaging, and marketing of carvings, etc.

Each year there is some discussion that fascinates me. Last year it was an illustration of the traditional Inuit concept of the primacy of the group over the individual, exemplified by Saati's efforts to resign from his job of delivering fuel. The Board pleaded that the community needed his services. He protested that he never had his sleep out without being awakened to make a delivery, a cogent argument bound to strike a sympathetic chord among the assembly of traditional hunters who value well-earned long sleep after a gruelling hunt. His wife added her lament that the aroma of oil permeated everything in their house, their clothes were ruined, and the expense as well as the labour was more than she could bear. After much discussion Atani volunteered to work throughout the winter with Saati, but only until warmer weather when he would resume his life as a full-time hunter and trapper. Later, both men were elected to the Board of Directors.

This year the use of alcohol held the attention of the assembly for some time. In the previous enclave society, every person in each group was interested in every aspect of the life of the group. Though one person might be judged a good sewer and another an excellent hunter, individuals — all aspects of whose lives were open to those around them — were seen as a whole, not merely as a hunter or a sewer of skins, but also as storyteller, housekeeper, moody or even-tempered, and so on. The people have welcomed the comforts and goods of a consumer society and the division of their lives into unrelated compartments. From non-natives they have learned to distinguish times to work and play, to differentiate public from private behaviour, and to count the days until the weekend.

This idea of privacy animated the Co-op discussion centred on the provision in the original bylaws prohibiting the consumption of alcohol by members. With the evolution of the Inuit society of Igloolik, in which sophisticated wage-earners order liquor from the South, should the proscription be disregarded, repealed, or enforced? As the original ideals of the Igloolik Eskimo Co-operative and its current practices were scrutinized, the stance of some members and advisors, who view co-operatives as no more than business institutions, conflicted with the more traditional idea of an Inuit organization legitimately concerned with the spiritual, moral, and physical well-being of its members.

The marathon session continued while I slipped out to relieve my burning eyes and assuage my growling stomach. With others, I returned to vote for the new Board members.

Throughout the meeting I again chafed at not being able to understand more of the discussion. The only learning method I have not tried is to dismiss any intention of mastering Inuktitut and just sink into the language and possibly osmote it. But alas! My temperament will not allow me to stop struggling to communicate. Even the Inuit now make excuses for my lack of proficiency, for they have seen how hard I try and how little I improve over the years. Diplomatically, older people tell me how they were in the sanatorium for a while but learned less of my language than I have of theirs. When they tell me I am too old to learn Inuktitut, I appreciate their sensitivity and tactfulness and I accept the compliment of being old as sugar coating for the bitter pill of my linguistic ineptitude.

If I am to be considered old, I wish I might be thought old enough to merit a house with running water . . . but how would I get used to a messy, built-in tile pocket for my bath soap instead of my free-standing, freely-dripping walrus vertebra?

6 January

Luncheon menu: caribou quarq, walrus aorta, macaroni and cheese.

At 11:30 Sila clambers up the snowbank between the road and the front steps of their pre-fab, four-bedroom house. She places her brown paper bag of Co-op groceries on the tiny porch and inspects the contents of the small, chest-type freezer half buried in the snowbank slowly building up along the front of the house. Unsatisfied with the freezer selection, she kicks about in the snow at the side of the house until she unearths a caribou neck, knocks the snow from it, and brings it and the groceries into the house. Larry and Angut's youngest pummel the meat, placed on a flattened cardboard box, on the floor between the kitchen and dining area, while Sila busies herself in the kitchen.

The noise of the two children is soon compounded by the arrival of the school children and adults for lunch. While Toby takes off the coveralls he wears while driving the sump truck and washes up, newlyweds Levi and Laura squat in their parkas savouring the raw, frozen meat. Sila is the recipient of smiles and nods as she adds a raw walrus aorta and a chunk of seal fat to the cardboard dining table. The children — nine of them now — run around, playing obstreperously between bites of the red meat and fat or chewy, whitish aorta fed to them by older children or adults. When the baby on Laura's back wriggles, it is bounced up enough for its mother to lean towards it and place chewed food directly into its mouth from hers. One of the school children discovers macaroni and cheese in a pot on the stove and the toddlers whine until fifth-grader Rebecca serves them in a metal plate. The youngest ones dig in with their fingers, spreading more on their faces than in their mouths, soon tire of the game, and return to the group of adults who cut more bites of meat for them.

As the adults finish, they leave the butcher knives and ulus by the meat to go and wash in the kitchen, then some help themselves to macaroni and cheese while others make coffee from hot water in an electric urn or pour tea from a kettle on the electric stove. By the time the caribou neck is tossed back outdoors into the snowbank and the aorta put into the refrigerator, Larry has fallen asleep on the couch, hugging a bottle of orange juice while Angut's little son, brandishing a bottle of evaporated milk thinned with tap water, pursues seven-year-old Sita in a game of their own invention.

12 January

At Sunday Mass the list of babies baptized last year and the names of the mothers was read. The use of more Inuktitut names instead of baptismal or husband's names in today's list, and at elections for the parish council and Co-op Board of Directors, is an indication of the local political climate.

The dark seemed particularly lovely this year for there were no long periods of bad weather. Often it was beautifully clear with crystalline stars and northern lights. The moon was spectacular, night after night rising enormous, orange with dark blue shadows on its face, which makes me think of Marcusi's tale.

"When I was a small boy living on the land, my baby brother died," he told me. "My father studied the face of the full moon with me, then pointed out the shadow of my deceased grandmother pulling my baby brother on a qamutik."

As the moon waned, it would hang pink against the twilight sky of midday. Often the snow and sky blended in rose and palest lavender as the sun rolled by under the horizon. One morning, from my doorstep, I watched a light for the longest time until I was convinced it was not that of a plane landing. It remained stationary, flashing white now and then but remaining red most of the time. It was a Saturday morning and a flock of snowmachines was heading across the bay as hunters went after walrus, so that I could compare this light with them to be sure it was not a tail light. It finally dawned on me that it was the planet Mars, spectacular against the pale blue and pink horizon with the rest of the heavens dark.

13 January

With the return of the sun we can expect the coldest temperatures of the year because, as Itu explained to me, the cold comes out of the ground rising towards the sun. I hear the school principal played the Beatles' record "Here Comes the Sun" over the school public address system in honour of the event. I wonder how many days it will take before the orange-red glob I saw just peeking over the hill this morning really begins to look like the orb our minds visualize when we speak of "the return of the sun." Last year was disappointing because of cloudy weather behind which Old Sol hid for over a week, until he at last appeared riding high and round. Maybe this year I can measure how much farther east it rises each day and much farther west it sets. My rough estimate is one giant step per day. Just as noticeable is the moon, barely dipping behind the land before starting to climb again, flushed red by the effort.

15 January

The recrudescence of the TB that has plagued Alitsiaq for years has again reduced her to a weakly smiling bundle of skin and bones. Her room reflects the concern of friends. On the walls are several picture calendars and two decorative mirrors. I took one from the wall and asked her which of the sea shells on the frame are from animals found in the land of the Inuit. I was surprised at how many she recognized as natives of the North. "Do you eat any of them?" She pointed out mussel and periwinkle shells and lost me in her dissertation on snails. Perhaps for lack of language skill, I have missed some gourmet recipe from the eaters-of-raw!

The bedside table is a profusion of bottles of pills of varying sizes and colours, an opened can of applesauce from which protrudes the handle of a spoon, china figurines, bottles of beads, a half a can of apple juice, dry and wet tissues, prayer books, a Bible, and candies, the whole brightened by the numerous blooms of a miniature marigold plant. Wanly smiling, the gentle Alitsiaq was sitting up on the bed, clothed in new pyjamas and surrounded by gaily covered pillows, gifts sewed by loving friends. On the floor next to the bed is a wastebasket into which she can spit.

Despite her wasted limbs she wields her ulu as daintily as ever, slicing off tasty cartilage from the raw caribou larynx on the plate before her on the patchwork quilt. She chewed slowly a long time before selecting a bit of fat and raw kidney. She seemed to enjoy the little she ate.

21 January

This is the day Marcusi escaped injury when the water truck rolled.

He was out early trying to make an extra run because so many people are low on water. At 6:30 A.M. he had just filled the tank at a house on the hill beyond me, when the brakes failed. He tried to run into a snowbank but hit a power pole which flipped the truck over. As the truck was dragged off towards the garage, the door on the driver's side was hanging off and the whole cab was twisted at a slight angle. Marcusi spoke on the radio at noon, chuckling and describing the accident, saying he was lucky to be alive and thanking God for taking care of him. I'm melting snow to wash my hair.

22 January

The ecumenical prayer service may yet become an annual event. Last year the church leaders met on neutral ground, in the school library, for Bible readings, hymns, and sermonettes. What I felt to be stiff may just have been the solemnity normal to a church service. This year the Catholic fathers and two of the Inuit lay helpers joined the Anglican minister, his assistants, and choir in a service at St. Matthias. Members of each congregation sang lustily as the selections alternated from one confession to the other. Catholic women gravitated towards the left-hand pews, their men to the right, just as they sit in the Catholic church; whereas more Anglicans sat together, many couples keeping their children with them instead of letting them huddle in the front rows, which soon became a wriggling mass of poking, playing youngsters. My distraction during the service was the realization that babies are not like dogs when it comes to howling. If one dog starts all the other join in, but it only *seems* as if the babies do the same in church. Several wailing Anglican tots were carried out by the monitor, who returned the silent child a few minutes later. The service seemed better organized this year, but when we emerged, the northern lights were very disorganized, floating all over the sky, appearing in tufts here and there instead of waxing and waning in their customary orderly fashion.

24 January

Today the local radio audience was invited to come pray at Inaq's house. After a hymn and reading of healing prayers, people crowded into Alitsiaq's room, each person praying simply and sincerely that the sick woman be able to eat and sleep, and that her husband Inaq and their children might also sleep and remain healthy.

25 January

There is a geologist from Yellowknife here to teach a course co-sponsored by Canada Manpower and the Territorial Government Continuing Education Department. The rationale is that hunters learning mineral identification can stake claims to sell or develop themselves, or hire on as claim stakers for companies exploring in their hunting areas. Last night there were four well advertised and well attended introductory movies. During the film on glaciation a bright young Inuk ostentatiously stomped out. He is typical of a number of people who can function in both societies. This young man quit a government training program and returned to live the life of a "real Inuk," hunting and trapping, while waiting for some official to beg him to accept a huge salary to again work for the government. This morning he accosted me with a scathing, "Do you believe that junk?" before delivering a vehement exposé of the falsehoods propagated by "that white man," the geologist. I laughed off the tirade saying I thought that today some of the older people were enjoying comparing the white man's creation myths with theirs. The Lab manager's wife and I were the only non-Inuit and also the only women who signed up for the course, which will meet five afternoons and evenings for two weeks.

26 January

The nurses tell me the tuberculosis X-ray films have turned up — in Cambridge Bay.

February

3 February

Since hunters here are also carvers and the people are alert to anything different on the land, it is not unusual to find collections of soapstone, other rocks, and fossils in their homes. About twenty men showed up for the first geology class and clustered around the geologist presenting him rocks, showing him on the maps where they came from, and asking him what they were worth. However the crowd simmered down to five faithful Inuit, all of whom evaporated tonight to attend a land claims discussion.

Inuit Tapirisat of Canada was founded in 1971 and led by aggressive young Inuit who perhaps perceived the potential for dangerous change through pressures from the qallunaak government in the North. Gradually, where they came to be known in southern Canada, their organization was accepted as the voice of the Inuit. But it was not until the November 1975 meeting at Pond Inlet that ITC aroused general interest among the people it supposedly represented. Until then most Inuit hunters dismissed land claims negotiations as merely some Inuit conducting esoteric word exercises with some white men. The Inuit were galvanized by the realization that the tasks might affect hunting — the basis of the lifestyle they wish to preserve. These past few weeks there have been meetings of committees and joint meetings of every committee in the settlement, all discussing ITC's proposed land claims settlement.

5 February

There has been blowing snow all day. The Nordair Twin Otter that brought the ITC men two days ago is still sitting on the airstrip, its two pilots and three mechanics at the Transient Centre. An engine came in for the mechanics on a DC-3 chartered yesterday to take the teachers out to their regional conference, held this year in Frobisher Bay.

This afternoon there was an Al Oeming movie at the school before our geology class. We did map work which drew in a crowd of moviegoers, including children, who milled around, forming groups around maps, swapping hunting and fishing tales, or plotting their travels. Two glasses set up for stereo viewing of the maps caused a sensation and were never unoccupied. The evening class was back to normal with only the old steadies in attendance.

What an impossible job to translate all those chemical reactions, geological terms different types of rocks, minerals, and land formations! Inuktitut, evolved in a hunting and gathering society preoccupied with survival, conveys the natural world around it. Even its myths are related in concrete terms: a woman controls the sea and its animals; the sun and moon are sister and brother immortalized. Though there are tales of hunting and dancing prowess, there was no need for conceptual terms or generic abstracts. There is a word for to sing, to beat the drum, to wail — but not for music. Objects can be described as red, blue, or yellow — but the word "colour" does not exist. Yet because it follows very definite rules of structure, Inuktitut readily lends itself to include new phenomena. Agglutinated words, which add qualifying parts of speech to a central idea, are understood the first time they are heard: the machine that dries clothes, the place where frozen food is kept, the person who deal with money.

In the case of mineral and rock identification, to mention but one façet of our course, the interpreter is faced with the task of furnishing an immediate description of substances that students spend many lab hours learning to identify. When you've used the term "like back fat" for the first white rock, what do you use for the next? Language committees are fashioning tools to deal with government, science, medicine, finance, petroleum and mineral exploration, technology, and more, but the geology vocabulary is not yet ready. After naming the first pink rock "char-red," how will the interpreter explain that the next pink rock differs in crystalline structure?

7 February

This is the last day of our prospecting and claim staking course, and I caught myself romanticizing the Inuit. The instructor admonished us to map finds to ensure being able to locate them again. My thought was, "These people have maps in their heads. They can find anything." Then I realized I was thinking of Inuit as "noble savages" instead of normal human beings with faults and virtues. What I was considering to be inborn superiority is the result of training.

I still have no water and continue to take my dirty dishes to the Transient Centre. The Co-op is cutting lake-ice blocks again this year and many people are getting leached sea ice. I have been scrounging, chunk by chunk, from the neighbours. Tomorrow I'll go over to Itu's for some. The water truck was on the road last week and delivered to the Transient Centre but collapsed again before it got to my part of town.

8 February

Cindy headed a procession of children bringing me ice and a fish from her husband's catch. There are ptarmigans over by the airstrip so I may have fish, fowl, and flesh all in the same week.

I watched as a teacher's wife served hot chocolate and cake to her children and a three-year-old Inuk playmate who repeated "ma-ma, ma-ma." The hostess was pleased that the little fellow was learning English, but couldn't figure out why he was calling her "mama." Perhaps because she has been in the North four years and I felt she should have known, I did not tell her that "ma-ma" is Inuktitut baby talk for mamaqtuq, "it tastes good." Her constant stream of "Don't spill," "Don't touch that," and "Be careful!" directed at her children as well as the visitor made me nervous. I may have been like that, almost harassing the kids, but I now try not to be because Inuit children don't have rules and taboos as white children do. Just last week I was proud of myself for remaining silent when a two-year-old climbed up, got a china cup off the table nd proceeded to dip out of the bucket where the ice melts by the stove. He rinsed the tea residue into the water, sprinkled the rug and floor, and might have broken the cup, but he didn't. A bit messy and unsanitary, but so what?

181

13 February

Last Monday I had a cold coming on so I took an antihistamine and went to bed at two in the afternoon. For the first time since I moved to Igloolik I felt sick enough to just lie in bed. At eight the next morning, when I dragged myself out and staggered over to the Transient Centre in a windy −40°, I found the kitchen drain frozen. Feeling very sorry for myself, I set about cooking breakfast and boiling water to pour on the pipes. As I rounded the corner of the building carrying the first pan to the outside pipe, I slipped on the smooth snow and splashed boiling water on my thigh. The burn immediately froze and the sink was more obstinate than usual. By the time breakfast was over my queasiness was cured. The cure didn't last, but at least I was launched into the day and now — four days later — the burn is streaked like a floor burn from my basketball playing days. The latest spot on my rump where I backed into the stove naked while bathing, is also healing nicely.

15 February

When I arrived at the Transient Centre, the thermostat needle was pressed against the lowest reading. One of the guests had phoned for help and taken refuge next door. By the time the coffee was perked, Timuti and Atani had arrived. Later, while waiting to see if the furnace was functioning properly, we ate toast, drank coffee, watched our breath, and played Crazy Eights. Atani remarked that it was as cold as a campsite where we had spent the night on the way to Ikpikitturjuaq.

17 February

The Commissioner's party of eleven will overnight here next Friday, the twenty-first. The construction company contracted to build the Nursing Station has finished the job and vacated the Transient Centre building they had leased. The furnace must have belched just before they left for you can write with your finger in the soot on the walls. I worked until almost midnight last night scrubbing the kitchen and pantry shelves and burning enormous amounts of French newspapers, including quite a few pornographic magazines and *Police Gazettes*. Today Mark's wife and two other women are over there washing walls. The electric line to the freezer is not working and the drains are all frozen. While I work in a frenzy and worry that the freezer will be warm and the pipes still frozen when the Commissioner's people arrive, the Inuit smile, relax, and everything will be done. Perhaps the airplane mechanic will be the one to fix the electricity and the Commissioner's secretary will thaw the drains, but it will be done, and probably everyone will be happy.

18 February

It was already getting light when I went to work at 7:30 A.M. but it is −45°C and the sun is not yet warm. Quite often the air has been still lately without a strong wind for some time and I really think we have smog.

In the south, dogs chase cars: today I chased trucks; oil trucks, water trucks, ice trucks. My fuel tank still has not been filled, possibly because I am just low, not out of oil; and I've taken advantage of a dry water tank to clean it. When I saw the fuel truck delivering on the row in front of mine, I scrambled into my kamiks, parka, and mitts and went over to ask the men to fill mine before it went dry. They were just pulling away as I got there and though I ran after them and waved, hoping they'd see me in the side mirror, it was to no avail. Less than an hour later, the water truck went by, and when it stopped at a house within sight I dashed after it. Marcusi sorrowfully proclaimed that he had just emptied the tank and he had to go for more water. I was lucky enough to get a ride out to the water lake and back. I mention "and back" because the new truck is laid up and it is by no means certain that this vehicle will complete a round trip without a side trip into the garage.

We waddled through the pressure ice onto the smoother frozen sea, then bumped back onto the land and continued to the spring water lake. My host leaped out when we got there and I discovered there was no handle on the right-hand door. I slid over to the driver's seat where I tried in vain to open the door. Then I gave a timid beep on the horn. No response. So I rolled the window down and climbed out. Marcusi was busy chipping away the ice over the water hole with an ice chisel on a handle almost six feet long. He used a dipper on an even longer handle to toss the ice fragments out onto the snow.

Three men drove off on motor toboggans just as I went to inspect the area where blocks of ice had been cut. One of them couldn't get rolling; his Yamaha would go a few yards then start spinning on the bare ice. Several times his towline broke. I tried pushing the qamutik when he started spinning, but when it still wouldn't budge I turned my back, intent on something else so as not embarrass him by seeming to notice his plight. There was a large chainsaw parked to one side of what looked like a huge swimming pool surrounded by ice blocks three feet high and two feet square. From a distance the sides of the swimming pool seemed black, but they faded to dark then light blue as one drew closer. The columns of ice around the hole were crystals of blue and bluish-green intricately veined with white. A couple of pairs of ice tongs and a chisel at least five feet long lay about, and occasional cigarette butts and yellow splotches on the snow also bore witness to the presence of man. It was a lovely scene in the bright sun under a faded blue sky. The white lake shaded into the white land and on the horizon the hummocky hills of Avvajja seemed like mountains hovering over the flatness of Igloolik.

When the tank truck was full, Marcusi put a plywood square over the water hole and a large chunk of snow on top of that. Then he shovelled enough snow on the plywood to barely cover it, probably so that the sun would not melt the board into the ice. As we left, the motor toboggans were returning with their empty sleds, followed by Simagak careening along in the Co-op truck. It was a lovely outing.

19 February

When I tried to answer a question Sila asked me about their phone bill, Toby kept trying — with minimal success — to have me do so in correct Inuktitut. Finally, he sighed resolutely, took pencil and paper and announced, "I'm going to teach you." It seemed like a good-natured threat implying, "and you'd jolly well better learn!" He and Sila are good teachers and I'm lucky they bother trying to teach me. He is more patient and makes fun of me less than she, but they both enjoy my gaffs and efforts. Their youngest talks quite well now and to think I knew him before he could walk, let alone talk. Will I never learn!

Maybe it was all the Inuktitut effort which caused me to loose a large filling. The nurses now have material to use for temporary fillings, so I'm fixed up for the nonce.

20 February

For each photographer that leaves, the next plane brings at least one replacement, all intent on photographing dog teams and smiling Inuit, their round faces framed in fur. Several Inuit keep caribou clothing at the ready and make a good living posing for photographers and taking them to the floe edge by dog team. However, after exposing much footage recording the approach of a splendid team yesterday, one photographer was chagrined to meet his subject — a local white resident, himself a professional photographer.

27 February

The sun is so bright the white chimney smoke is casting shadows, but −35° is still too cold for my nose. Marcusi has blossomed forth with the twin of my parka fur. The ruff on his new parka is from the beautiful grey dog skin I'm wearing for the second season.

The Commissioner *did* come, the Transient Centre *was* ready, and it was a very profitable trip for me. They arrived on a chartered Twin Otter which returned to Frobisher Bay taking me along. The dentist filled my tooth on Saturday morning and I returned home on the Monday sched, carrying a baby home to his mother in Hall Beach and escorting a frisky five-year-old back to Igloolik. I did lots of visiting for such a short time. One of the public health nurses told me there is no TB carrier in Igloolik and gave me some outdated birth control pills to use as fertilizer for my plants.

28 February

The minutes of the meeting the Commissioner held with the settlement council last week sparked an animated discussion this evening at our University of Saskatchewan cross-cultural education class. The minutes read in part:

> The Council explained that the education in Igloolik is very poor. That if you take a Grade 8 student and put him in Grade 8 in Ottawa, the student from Igloolik would look more like a Grade 5 student. The Commissioner explained to Council that the students just follow the path of their teachers. The Commissioner also said that the Council can nominate a person to be put on the board to help select the new principal for Igloolik. The Council

also explained that the students today are too free. Also that the teachers are too easy on the students. The Council also thinks that what the problem is, is that the students are learning two things at the same time, and that must be confusing for the students. So the Council suggests that out of one week, there should be at least two days of cultural inclusion. The Commissioner also explained that the problem is all over Canada. Also that the teachers are not to blame for this. This is because the teachers are just following, what the Department of Education tells them to do. He also said that the Territorial Council is trying to change the law of the Education. So that the local settlements will have more participation in taking care of the school and selecting a school principal and other things.

First of all, the class found the minutes themselves confusing and spent some time wondering what was meant by "following the path of teachers," and other ambiguous passages. Next was a long analysis of the contradictory positions: teach the students the same things that students in Ottawa learn and devote two days a week to cultural-inclusion instruction in syllabics and traditional hunting and homemaking skills.

Finally, to have Inuit complain that "the students today are too free" stunned the whites who charge that the Inuit refuse to discipline their children, and though the teachers are expected to do so, the parents complain every time their child is corrected or even scolded for coming to school late. The sporadic attendance of many of the children and the chronic tardiness of others were defined as the greatest impediments to effective teaching in Igloolik. The teachers who have been in the North the longest were the most dismayed.

Perhaps the worst blow was that the spokesman for the settlement was the Chairman of the Education Advisory Committee. "Why didn't he tell us?" asked the teachers. The staff here feel that they are doing a good job, serving the people well, and as individuals are conscientious, dedicated, and enthusiastic. From my more objective position, I see an eager group of teachers beavering away, oblivious to the confused observers puzzling to understand all the happy activity they see, and worrying about what it might be doing to their children. I am surprised by the surprise of the teachers that they have not won the hearts of the people, or at least their approbation and permission to exercise their specialty without being called to account.

March

3 March

Icicles drop long and thick from the eaves of the Hudson's Bay store. Fall and spring creatures they, formed only when the sun is warm and the air cold, so I guess it is spring.

The normal solution to the problem of springtime's slippery-soled kamiks is ujjuk rosettes like the ones Anna sewed on the soles of mine. More interesting is the broken zipper one woman put on her footwear, but most colourful are the knitted slippers several woman and children are sporting over their kamiks.

Siaku has built a porch of snow blocks around the back door of the store, carpenters in qulittaqs climb up to their work on the roofs of the new houses by way of snowbanks, and a toddler bundled up in a caribou romper suit neatly closed with a zipper is perhaps symbolic of the hope for the future of the North — that the best of each culture may merge for the good of the people.

5 March

Since the airstrip cannot accommodate planes larger than a DC-3, the hamlet has built a long strip on the ice in front of the settlement to enable a Hercules freighter to bring in a new generator for the Northern Canada Power Commission plant. The strip immediately became a highway and playground. From its far side, a road cuts across the ice, then back onto the land to the spring water lake — a road much frequented by pedestrians and vehicles from bikes to snowmachines taking fishermen out to the lake at all hours of the day and night.

One of the ladies of the qallunaak community is pregnant. I was made aware of the anticipated birth when she blossomed forth in full smocks over a still small front. She is now in her seventh month, quite weary of the wait, and complaining of how slowly the time is passing. She confided that the nurse had scolded her for not coming in sooner for pre-natal care and she had answered, "I subtracted the first months when I didn't go in for check-ups from the nine so I won't feel pregnant for such a long time."

Inuit woman don't feel womanly unless they have a baby in the amauti, and when they are too old to bear children they adopt them. Mothers make tiny amautis for little girls shortly after they have learned to walk, and the tots stuff dolls or puppies into them until they are big enough to carry the youngest baby of the family. It is not uncommon to see a five-year-old proudly staggering around with baby brother, sister, or cousin on her back. Nor is it surprising — since motherhood is the normal occupation of Inuit women — that the girls start having babies when they are fourteen and fifteen years old. Their Christian parents say, "Tut-tut," then beam at the prospect of a new baby and gleefully decide who shall have it. One year, when half the eighth grade was pregnant and the other half male, we white people theorized about the possibility of an Inuit attitude comparable to that of some South Pacific islanders who sent the girls out from the village at their first menstruations to come back only when they became pregnant, thus proving their eligibility for marriage. We wondered if having borne a child gave status to the local school girls.

Inuit cannot understand that anyone, particularly an older person, would want to live alone. Friends continue to offer me a child "to keep you company and take care of you now that you're getting old."

When an Inuk is pregnant, if the baby is not to be given to a friend or relative for adoption, there is usually its immediate predecessor to be weaned from breast to bottle. Only a few of the younger women wear maternity and nursing garments and the amauti can be worn until delivery, though the nurses counsel against carrying a baby in the pouch during the last few weeks.

This will be the qallunaak's second child. Some of my Inuit friends have ten children to care for, skins to scrape, furs to prepare, mittens, boots, and clothes to fashion, and they remark only that they tire faster doing skins and other chores. Women who have had miscarriages, difficult births, and other medical problems, are sent to Frobisher Bay, but others may deliver in the settlements. Most qallunaak women prefer to have their babies "at home," (in the south) and among those who choose to give birth in the villages, for one reason or another, almost all are sent by the local nurses to the nearest hospital in Frobisher Bay.

8 March

Maybe it's not the temperature extremes that have been killing my plants, but those birth control pills. . . .

There was a huge rainbow ring around the sun when I came back from the Co-op this morning. Where the circle touched the horizon, there was a large spot of light, rising from the earth like a bright white dome against a pale blue sky, and tonight there is a green corolla. I noticed it as I stepped out to empty wash water, and I stayed out enjoying it after every bucket of water until my nose told me to go in.

15 March

The children have been warned not to dig dens in the snowbanks at the bottom of the bluffs on either side of the settlement, for fear sliders or motor toboggans will fall into them.

It is −10° C and, with the warm weather and snow blowing from the northeast, my window is a kinetic painting. Two ice lumps between the panes have expanded throughout the season, developing clear cores from the sun's warmth through the outside pane and the heat from the stove working from the inside. The edges of the lumps, pressing against both panes, have been eaten into lace by the heat. Sheets and ridges of clear ice, where meltwater has been able to run freely until caught by the cold, reflect the light. Winds bring snow of the finest texture to cling to the forms beneath the panes, building mounds along the casements and cracks through which it enters. At night, in the stillness, the window emits spring noises: tinkles as bits of ice between the panes chip off; rustles of sliding droplets; clicks of tiny collisions. Blue sky appears in arches as the ice cover retreats, and the black tape holding the broken glass into its frame slashes across the pale, glittering canvas of my window.

I am becoming a farmer, or at least I hope I am. I am more and more content to plant seeds knowing that I may not — indeed, probably will not — see the results. This year I have visited often with whites and I realize how much I have changed during my few years north of the tree line. Am I learning patience? Or acquiring the wisdom to know what must be changed and what may remain as it is? I no longer chafe about planes. Though I can still rant and rave about inadequate or misplaced air service, I do so not because it bothers me personally, but because of the impediment the poor transportation presents to the control of the North by northerners. Plane service, which brings mail and transports passengers and freight, is an umbilical cord attaching most whites to their homes in the South. For me, home is North. Often now, I find myself explaining some Inuit attitude, or justifying some Inuit action to one of my qallunaak friends or, even more often, just shrugging off the whole episode. But I well remember reacting exactly as they do. Is my attitude the beginning of that patience and gentleness that struck me as the hallmark of so many of the missionaries who had spent long years among the Inuit? I hope so, but. . . .

Glossary

Spelling is the proposed standard orthography endorsed by all Inuit and northern government agencies. In addition to the Roman alphabet, £ (the symbol for the pound sterling) is sounded somewhat like "sl."

Words are given in the Igloolik dialect and may be different in other settlements.

AGLU   Seal breathing hole

AJAGAQ   A game in which a vertebra of caribou, walrus, or other large animal, or the skull of rabbit, fox, or other small animal, is attached by a length of cord to a rib bone. The large bone is tossed and caught on the rib while a line of narrative is recited, each player trying to complete the story verses without missing.

AJURNAQTUQ   It is difficult (one of many possible meanings)

AJURNARMAT   It can't be helped (one of many possible meanings)

AS£UNAAQ   Rope made of bearded seal skin

AMAUTI   Inuit woman's outer garment with a pouch in which to carry a baby and a hood to pull over the head in very cold or stormy weather. The inner garment is made of duffel, blanket material or caribou skin and the outer shell of Grenfell or other heavy fabric. The outer shell is decorated with rick-rack or braid.

ARVIQ   Greenland or right whale

ATII   Go ahead, keep on (two of many possible meanings)

AVATAQ   Sealskin float to attach to a harpooned animal

AVINNGAQ   Lemming

CHAR   Pink fish of the trout family

IGLIQ   Sleeping platform, bed

IGUNAQ   Fermented meats and fish aged the Inuit way

INUIT (pl.)   Plural of Inuk, "the People"

INUK (sing.)   "One of the People"

INUKTITUT   Language of the Inuit

ISUMA   Intelligence; name spirit

KAKIVAK   Trident fish spear with straight, short centre prong and two longer, pliable outside prongs bending in, thus allowing the fish to enter but impaling it when it backs out.

KAMIKS   Women's short boots with sealskin soles and cloth tops with braid and/or rick-rack design around the upper cuff. The word is coming to be used, particularly by non-Inuit, to designate all Inuit footwear.

MAKTAAQ   Beluga and narwhal skin

MAKTAK   Greenland or right whale skin

NATIQ   Ring seal

NUGLUKTAQ   Thread-the-spear. An object with a hole in it — a vertebra or carved piece of bone or ivory — is hung from the dome of the iglu or from a ceiling. Players, each with a pointed stick or spear, encircle the dangling target, and, at the command, all try to be the first to impale the object.

ORIENTAL SPOT   A temporary blue birthmark at the base of the spine

PARKA   Formerly the duffel coat with Grenfell cloth outer shell that replaced skin clothing with the advent of traders. Now both the hand-sewn duffel and manufactured garments with a hood designed for cold weather.

PATIK   A gambling card game

PILOT BISCUIT   Large, hard, unsalted biscuit

QALLUNAAQ (sing.)   White man or woman

QALLUNAAT (pl.)   White men or women

QAMUTIK   Inuit sled from eight to twelve feet in length and three to four feet wide, consisting of twelve-inch-high runners lashed to crossbars.

QARMAT   Formerly a whale bone and sod house, later a sod house

QUARQ   Frozen raw meat or fish

QUJANA   Too bad! Tough!

QULLIQ   Half-moon shaped lamp, usually carved of steatite, with seal or whale fat fuel and cotton grass wick. Used for light and for cooking.

QULITTAQ   Man's caribou-skin parka, fur out

TUGAALIK   Tusked narwhal

UJJUK   Bearded or square-flipper seal whose skin is used for boot soles and thongs

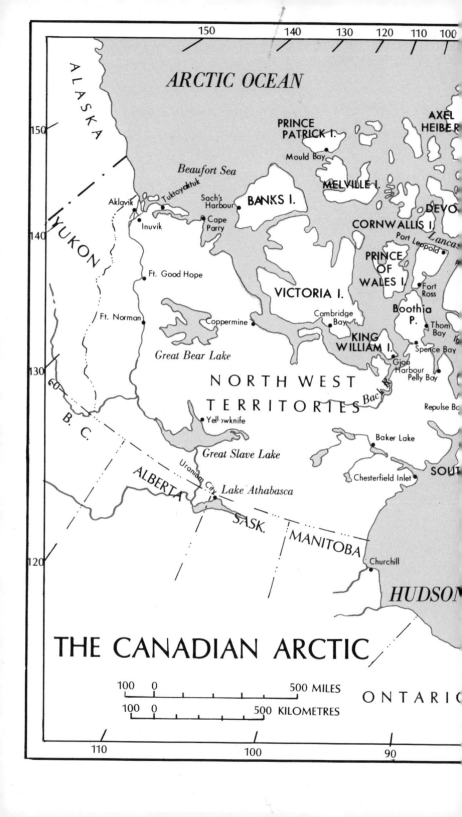

THE CANADIAN ARCTIC